# BASILDON
## A Pictorial History

# BASILDON
## A Pictorial History

*by*

## JESSIE K. PAYNE B.A.

## Phillimore

1981

Published by
PHILLIMORE & CO. LTD.
London and Chichester

*Head Office*: Shopwyke Hall,
Chichester, Sussex, England

ISBN 0 85033 366 0

*Dedicated to
the memory of my father
Alfred John Moss*

Printed and bound in Great Britain by
GARDEN CITY PRESS, LTD.
Letchworth, Herts.

# Illustrations

# Preface & Acknowledgements

Until the turn of the century Basildon was just a collection of small villages, with quiet roads and lanes, ancient farmhouses and cottages that had changed little over the centuries. The illustrations in this volume are intended to give some idea of what it was like before the coming of the New Town. After 1900 the first sporadic growth began, and much farm land was turned into building plots for the tiny timber bungalows, so popular as week-end retreats for Londoners in the 1920s and 1930s.

This cannot be a full history of Basildon, though there is much to record. There is evidence of Paleolithic and Mesolithic sites at Vange, and a Bronze Age hoard was found in 1953 on the site of Swan Mead School. There was a Romano-British farm in Lee Chapel Lane; but the name Basildon (and those of the other villages in the district also covered by this book: Bowers Gifford, Langdon Hills, Laindon, Lee Chapel, Nevendon, Pitsea, Vange and parts of Dunton and North Benfleet), is of Saxon origin.

The inventory of the Royal Commission on Historical Monuments 1923 lists 18 buildings other than the parish churches and of these seven remain. These and other old buildings that still exist are pictured here because of their long and interesting histories, but many more pictures illustrate the numerous houses, shops and farms (and the people that lived in them) that disappeared and were swallowed up in the growth of the New Town.

This book has been a joy to prepare, for I knew and loved old Basildon. Although many of the photographs have come from my collection, this book would not have been possible without the help so generously given by many people.

I particularly wish to thank the Basildon Corporation and Mrs. P. Hayes of the Information and Publicity Office for their unfailing help and courtesy in providing information and obtaining pictures; Mr. P. R. Lucas of Basildon Council; Mr. N. D. Humphries of Basildon Central Library; Mr. V. W. Gray, the County Archivist and his staff at the Essex Record Office; the Phaidon Press for permission to use the picture of the Bayeux Tapestry; The Public Record Office for permission to use the Domesday Extract for Barstable Manor; *The Southend Standard* and *The Basildon Recorder* for permission to use photographs; Mr. A. E. Blandford, Editor of *The Basildon Recorder* and Mr. A. Paffey for the photograph of the graves of the Hornsby tombstones; Mr. W. Whiting for making an excellent copy from a decaying photograph; Mr. Wright of the Cater Museum for copying the photograph of Major Spitty; The Langdon Hills Conservation Society; Mr. G. Williams for photographs and information and Mr. I. Johnstone for help with photography.

I am also much indebted to all those who so kindly loaned me photographs, especially Mr. A. E. Campbell; Mr. F. Clark; Miss P. Cook; Mrs. M. D. Doodes; Mrs. D. Ellis; Miss W. Chataway; Miss E. Norman; Dr. Warwick Rodwell; Mrs. E. Treeton; Mr. A. Waylett; Mr. C. Wicker; the late Mrs. B. Wyatt.

# Abbreviations

| | |
|---|---|
| E.A.S.T. | Essex Archaeological Society Transactions |
| E.R.O. | Essex Record Office |
| NS | New Series |
| QSR | Quarter Sessions Rolls |
| R.C.H.M. | Royal Commission on Historical Monuments |
| V.C.H. | Victoria County History of Essex |

# I Domesday Entry

## BARSTABLE MANOR IN THE DOMESDAY BOOK

Domesday Book was compiled in 1086. This is one example from the entries for the Basildon area.

### Translation

Berdestapla (Barstable) which was held by a freeman as 5½ hides [hide=120 acres] and 30 acres is held of the Bishop [Odo of Bayeux] by Ralph the son of Turold. And there are 30 acres of wood(land) and pasture for 100 sheep. Then [1066] as now 3 ploughs [8 oxen per plough] on the desmesne and 2 belonging to the men. There are 6 villeins and 11 bordars. It was then worth 4 pounds, now 100 shillings. There were then in the desmesne 2 rounceys [horses], 5 beasts [non ploughing oxen], 18 swine and 36 sheep; now 1 rouncey, 9 beasts, 24 swine and 80 sheep.

# II Chapman & Andre's Map

2. Chapman and Andre's Map, 1777. Honey Pot Lane is shown as a parish road with Little Barstable Hall, which was the site of the town centre, leading from it. Further north is Sawyers, the scene of the murder of Mr. and Mrs. Watson 1906. Middle Hall, a small farm, is shown midway between Vange Hall and Basildon Hall, hence the name. Shophouse Farm and the windmill are shown off Rectory Road, Pitsea. Landmarks remaining are the *Five Bells*, Vange, Chalton (Chalvedon) Hall, Pitsea and Fobbing Farm.

# III Early History of Manors

It is not possible in a book of this description to give more than a fleeting glance at some of the noble, famous and interesting people who held the land in the New Town area in medieval days.

One of the greediest landowners at the time of the Domesday Survey in 1086 was Odo, Bishop of Bayeux, the half brother of the Conqueror. He assisted William at the Battle of Hastings and was richly rewarded with 216 lordships, among them a manor at Vange and another (Barstable) at Basildon (T. Wright, *History and Topography of Essex*, 1835). Odo's tenant at Vange was Ralph, son of Turold, who was another land grabber. He and Odo are portrayed in the Bayeux Tapestry.

Some of the manors in the area were held by monasteries or the church. Laindon was held by the Bishop of London from the time of the Domesday Survey. Ulveva, the wife of Phin the Dane held Pitsea at that time. Phin was apparently a man of some importance who held land elsewhere in Essex. Soon after the Survey Pitsea passed to Eudo Dapifer, the Norman steward of the Conqueror. Eudo gave part of Pitsea (Pitsea Hall) to the great abbey of St. John, Colchester. The remaining part of Pitsea (Chalvedon Hall) came into the possession of Ailward, the King's chamberlain in 1177. By 1278 Chalvedon was held by the Priory of St. Mary Spittle, London (E.A.S.T., Vol. XVII, NS p. 18). This priory was founded by Walter Brune, one of the sheriffs of London and Rosia his wife. Spital Fields takes its name from it (*Encyclopaedia of London*, William Kent, p. 69). The same priory came into the possession of Great Bromfords, Nevendon about the time of Henry V. Westminster Abbey also held land at Bowers Gifford at the time of the Domesday Survey.

Another important landholder in Basildon after the Conquest was Suen, Sheriff of Essex whose castle was at Rayleigh. He held Botelers or Belesdon manor and Bertlesden or Battleswick in Basildon, the last named was near Holy Cross Church but cannot now be identified, and also Langdon Hills Manor.

Besides Westminster Abbey, Walter the Deacon and Grim the Reeve, who was an Englishman, held land at Bowers Gifford at the time of the Domesday Survey. It afterwards passed through the hands of the Mantel, Layborn, Sutton and Bygod families to the Norman family of Gifford who were descended from the same family as the Conqueror. The Giffords held it for about a century and gave their name to the parish.

In the Middle Ages the great de Vere family whose splendid castle still exists at Castle Hedingham, Essex held Botelers (Moat Farm) in Basildon also Vange and Bowers Gifford after the Gifford family.

From the de Veres Vange passed through the hands of Valence, Earl of Pembroke, and the families of Rede and Wetenhale. In 1457 William Wetenhale, citizen and alderman of London held Vange by the service of one silver needle of the price of two pence.

At the Reformation both Pitsea manors passed from monastic hands to Thomas, Lord Cromwell. On his attainder in 1540 both manors were assigned as part of the maintenance of the Princess Mary (afterwards Queen Mary). Queen Elizabeth granted them to Thomas Howard, Duke of Norfolk and upon his execution in 1572 on account of his involvement with the affairs of Mary Queen of Scots, the manors were forfeited. Chalvedon was, however, restored to his son, Thomas, Lord Howard created Earl of Suffolk 1603 and later passed to the Prescot family. Pitsea Hall passed to his eldest son Philip Howard, Earl of Arundel. In 1664 Samuel Moyer an eminent merchant held Pitsea Hall. His son a rich Turkey merchant was sheriff of Essex in 1698 and created a baronet in 1701.

At Nevendon when the Priory of St. Mary Spittle was dissolved Great Bromfords passed to the Petre family whose descendents still live at Ingatestone Hall, Essex. Sir William Petre who bought Great Bromfords in the fifth year of Elizabeth was a remarkable man who served four sovereigns holding office continuously through all the uncertainties of the reigns of Henry VIII, Edward VI, Mary and Elizabeth, escaping execution, imprisonment, dismissal and disgrace.

The FitzLewis family were the lords of the manor of Little Bromfords, Nevendon until the middle of the 16th century.

Langdon Hills manor was given to the University of Oxford by Thomas White DD. as part of the endowment of the five scholarships and professorships of moral philosophy which he founded in 1621.

One parish in the area which disappeared in the middle ages was Westley; only the name, Westley Hall, remains. This before the Conquest was held by Edeva the Queen of Edward the Confessor. It then passed into the hands of the Dean and Chapter of St. Pauls. Westley was united to Langdon Hills in 1432 owing to the poverty of the two parishes.

3.   The Bayeux Tapestry, showing one of the earliest landlords of Basildon,
Odo, Bishop of Bayeux. This section shows Duke William of Normandy in
council with Odo (seated on his right), ordering the building of the invasion
fleet. Bishop Odo received two manors in the Basildon area after the Battle
of Hastings.

4.   Sir John Gifford, lord of the manor of Bowers Gifford, 1348. The brass
in Bowers Gifford Church is the last brass surviving in England showing an
armament almost exclusively of mail (E.A.S.T. Vol. XXII NS pp. 276-298).
During the reign of Edward II, Roger de Wodeham, Constable of Hadleigh
Castle raided the manor of Bowers and would have killed Sir John had he
found him (E.A.S.T. Vol. I p.94-5).  In 1345 Sir John went on pilgrimage
to Santiago de Compostella in Spain (E.R.O. Calendar of Close Rolls).

5.  Moat Farm or Botelers, Basildon. It stood to the south of Holy Cross Church on the east side of Church Road. The land is now a recreation ground and the fine moat from the farm remains. At the time of the Domesday Survey it was known as Belesdon and was held by Suen of Essex who built Rayleigh Castle (P. Morant, *History of Essex*, 1768). During the 14th century it was held by the Travers family (E.R.O. D/DHf/T/46). John Boteller or Botill (Butler) appears to have married into the family, holding the property in 1362 and giving his name to the manor. In 1848 it was sold to the tenant Raynham for £5,160, and it was in his possession that the buildings burnt down (P. Benton, *History of Rochford Hundred*).

6.  (*opposite above*) Basildon or Barstable Hall. The house has been demolished and the moat was drained in October 1961. The dry moat can still be seen to the south of the housing at East Thorpe and Clickett Hill. The New Town centre has been built not far from this, the old Barstable Manor, which occupied an almost central position in the hundred to which it gave its name. The hundred was the Saxon division of a shire or county and its meeting place was the hundred moot. The Hall was probably the meeting place of the Barstable moot. 'Stapol' means post or pillar and suggests a meeting place and 'Bar' may either represent a personal name or the description of the post (P.H. Reaney, *Place Names of Essex*). The Sandells were lords of the manor until 1605 when John Lake of North Benfleet, who had married Elizabeth Sandell about 1589, bought it for £1,121 (W.G. Davis, *Ancestry of Bethia Harris 1748-1833*). During the agricultural depression following the Napoleonic Wars there were outbreaks of machine breaking and incendiarism and in 1830 property worth £3,000 was destroyed at Basildon Hall (reply to letter from John Moore by C. Comyns Parker, E.R.O. W/DOP B123/522-9).

7.  (*opposite below*) Barstable Cottage, sometimes called Hotwater Hall, standing at the end of Hotwater Lane. This appears to have been the house or its successor, mentioned by Morant as the house in the lower situation to which the farmer moved from Barstable Hall. He wrote . . . 'the mansion house (Barstable Hall) was a forlorn, weather-beaten edifice on rising ground deserted for another house in a lower situation with good water, where the farmer now dwelt' (P. Morant). It occupied the site of Northgate House in the town centre. The manor courts were probably held here and it is suggested that those summoned here were in 'hot water'. Basildon Hall remained within its moat and was rebuilt.

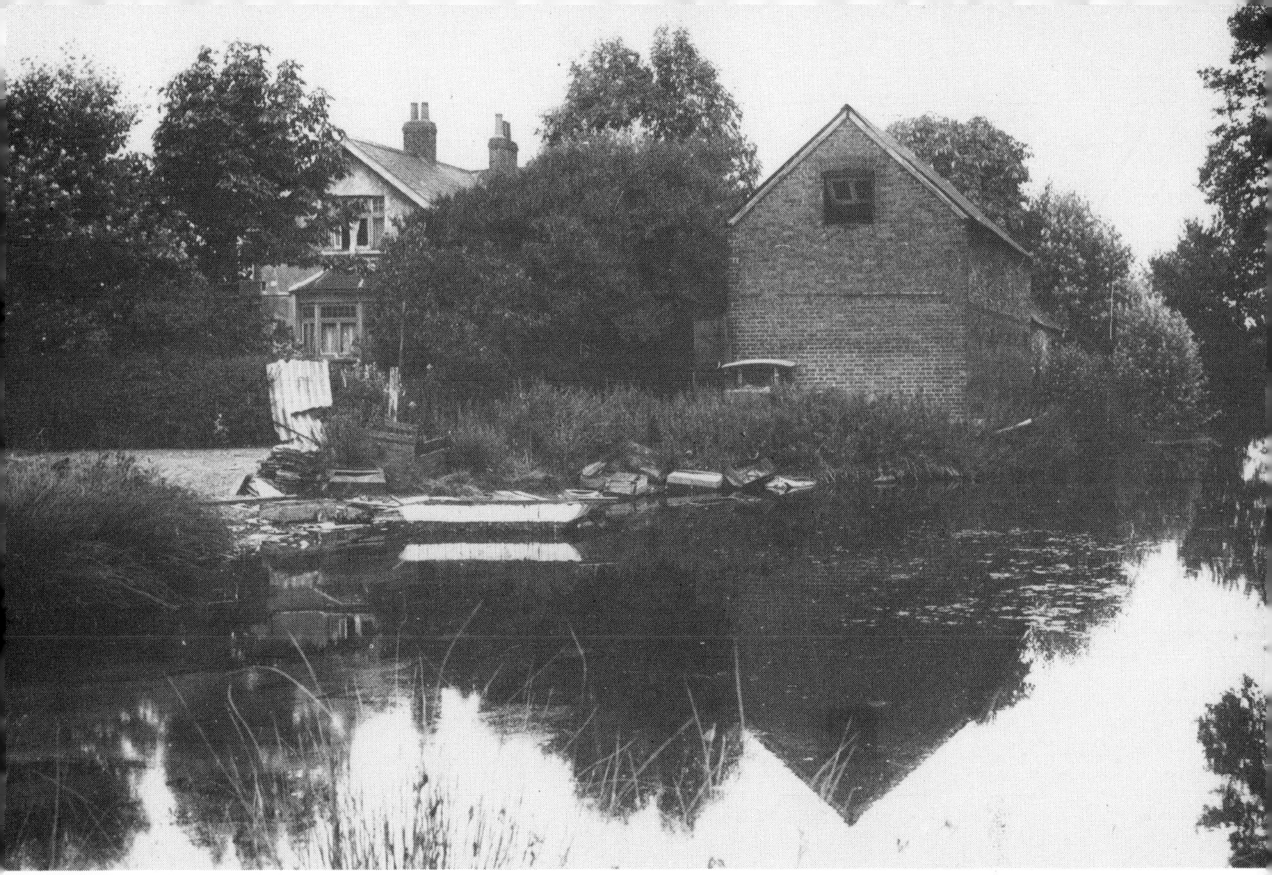

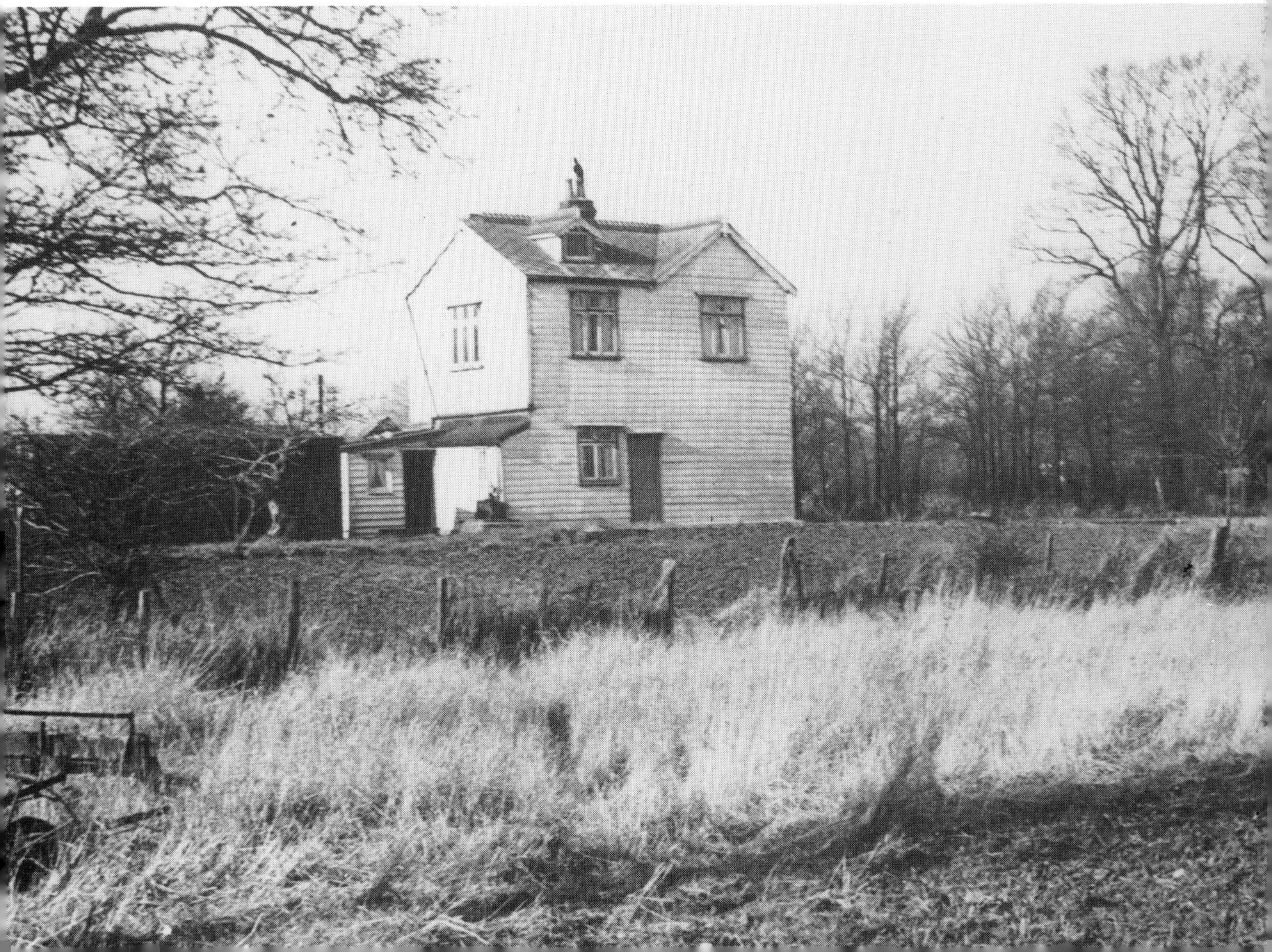

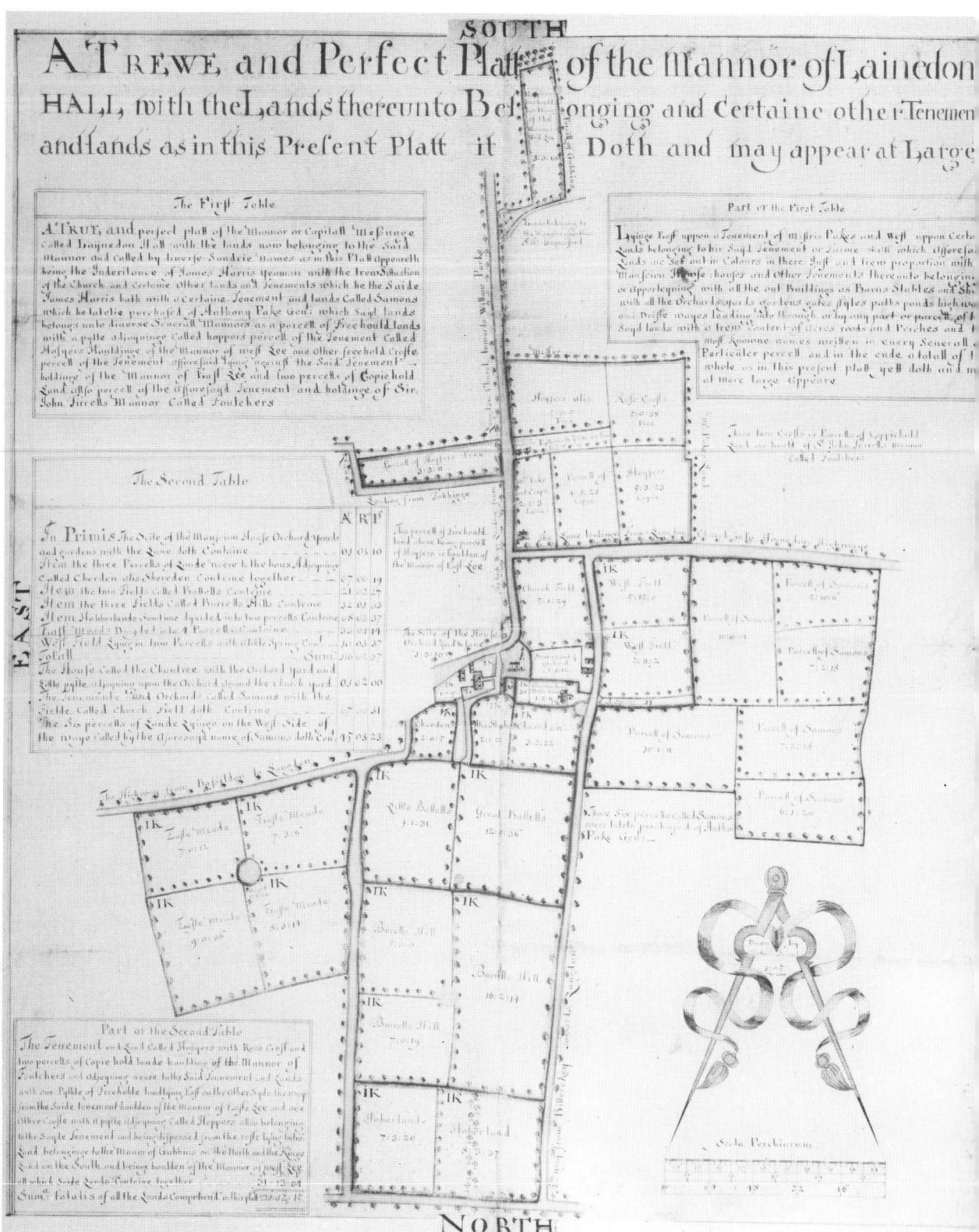

8. A plan or map of Laindon Hall Manor of 1707, purporting to be an exact copy of a map of c.1600. James Harris who lived in Laindon Hall (to the east of the church) had recently purchased the house and land called Samons. The house, with an orchard, can be seen to the west of the church abutting on Pound Lane. The house to the north-west the church, 'The Chantre', would appear to be the messuage mentioned with 95 acres of arable and 13s. 4d. rent, with which Thomas de Berdefeild endowed the chantry he founded in 1329 (P. Morant).

9. Laindon Hall. The farm stood to the east of St. Nicholas Church in St. Nicholas Lane. The lords of the manor were the Bishops of London but the Hall itself was occupied by farmers. The house was probably built in the 15th century. Carved and moulded pendants at the lower end of the gables, and carved and moulded tie beams dated from the Elizabethan period. Inside, moulded ceiling beams and in some rooms the original timber framed partitions could be seen with plastered spaces between the framing. There were two huge chimneys and the open fireplace in the kitchen had been altered to suit modern requirements. There was also the remains of a dairy (R.C.H.M. Vol. IV).

10. Laindon Hall, the north view. Basildon Council was considering turning it into a museum when it was destroyed by fire in 1964.

11. The lovely Elizabethan oak staircase of Laindon Hall. In 1593, while James Harris and his family slept, John Harding, a labourer, broke into the Hall. He was found guilty of stealing a doublet worth 10s., a pair of hose worth 5s., and 5s. in money (E.R.O. Assize File 36H). The church registers record that Elizabeth Braid, wife of James Braid, died at Laindon Hall in December 1784, aged thirty (E.R.O. OD/P 278/1).

12. The Manor House or Great Gubbins, Laindon, early this century. Great Gubbins is a corruption of Gobions from the Gobion family, one of the greatest landholding families in the area from the 13th to the 14th century. Manor Road led to the house, the site of which is now the recreation ground. In 1837 Great Gubbins was sold at the Auction Mart near the Bank of England. It was described as being 'in fine corn country with a brick farmhouse with tiled roof, two garrets, four bedrooms, a dressing room, two good parlours, store room and kitchen with convenient cellars, a lean-to brewhouse, and a wash-house and dairy with two apartments over, timber built and tiled'. The oak timber and tiled barn had an oak threshing floor (E.R.O. D/DOP B10/4). The ancient cellars may have been part of a previous homestead. On the right of the photograph is part of the moat.

13. Lee Chapel Farm. The site is now approximately covered by Gainsford in Lee Chapel South. Lee Chapel was an extra parochial liberty and paid no due to any parish, but was in the jurisdiction of the Constable of Laindon and was charged for taxes in that parish until it became a parish in the old Billericay Union. The manor was held by the Bohun family and in the reign of Henry VIII, the 3rd Duke of Buckingham held it. When he was beheaded for treason in May 1521, East Lee, as it was then known, reverted to the Crown. It passed through the hands of several families and in the 17th century it came to the Petre family (P. Morant). The house was destroyed by fire in 1915. Built of timber and brick in two parts, the back of the house probably dated from the 16th century and the front from the 18th century. This picture shows the older part of the house. The chalk footings of an earlier medieval structure were discovered on the site in 1964.

14. Another view of the farm, showing the front. To the nor of the farm, stood the chapel which gave its name to the paris of Lee Chapel, now part of the New Town. In 1848 there was no church or inn and only 11 inhabitants (White's *Gazetteer o Essex*, 1848). There is mention of Roger, the parson of 'Estle in 1248 (*Essex Review*, Vol. LI p. 159). Faint traces of the chapel were still said to exist in 1926 and in 1964 when building began in the vicinity of Gainsfords, rammed flint and chall footings were found. These comprised a rectangular building with due east-west orientation and the east end appeared to be apsidal. These were almost certainly the remains of a 12th-century chantry chapel or one that became one within a short space of time (information from Dr. Warwick Rodwell).

15.  Pitsea Hall.  The family of Alfred Baker farmed the land at the turn of the century.  The house dates from *c.*1600 (R.C.H.M. Vol. IV).  In the 18th century the village pound for straying cattle stood near the house (P. Morant), and manor courts were held at the hall up to the 19th century.  When repairs were being carried out here about thirty years ago, part of what was believed to be a subterranean passage was discovered. Damp timber props and some pottery were found and the passage was explored for a short distance.  It was quite erroneously believed to lead to Hadleigh Castle, but was probably an ancient drain.  In the 1960s the kitchen still had a stone floor, hooks for hams and an old bakers' oven.  Smuggling was carried on here and the contraband goods hidden in a pit in the yard and a huge kennel with a fierce dog placed over it.  (Information from the late Georgina Moss, whose mother was a Miss Baker.)

16.  The hunt meets at Great Bromfords in 1933.  The house which stood on the Nevendon-Wickford Road was built in the 15th century (R.C.H.M. Vol. IV).  It contained a priest's hole and was originally surrounded by a moat.  The name is probably associated with Roger de Brontford, Brunford, or Brumford, 1254 (P. H. Reaney).  The house was damaged by enemy action during the last war and was demolished about 1951.

17. (*top left*) Great Chalvedon Hall, Pitsea, about 1933. A chapel was founded at Chalvedon by Ailward, Chamberlain of Henry II, between 1177 and 1179. He was granted a licence by Abbot Walter and the Convent of Colchester who held the advowson of Pitsea Rectory (E.A.S.T. Vol. XVI, NS p. 115 and Vol. XVII, NS p. 18). There was a chapel field to the east of the house which might have been part of the endowment and was not necessarily the site of the chapel (Pitsea Tithe Map E.R.O. D/CT 274). A market and fair was held at Chalvedon in 1274 (Rotuli Hundredorum Vol. I, p. 154). From Tudor days the hall was inhabited by yeomen farmers. John Purland of 'Chandon Hall' was a Churchwarden but this did not prevent him from carting oats on Candlemas Day for which he was reported to the Archdeacon's Court in 1597 (E.R.O. Brownes Archdeaconry Transcripts). In St. Michael's Church, Pitsea, there is a brass inscription to Elizabeth, the wife of John Purlevant, who was buried in the Chancel in 1588. 'Purlevant' is no doubt a variation of Purland.     18. (*top right*) Vange Hall, 1955. Mrs. K. Moss, wife of the last tenant, is standing in the garden. The house overlooked the golf course, and although it did not appear to be very old it really was of great antiquity. The brick front was originally of wood and a 16th-century metal plate was found on an old door. Clement Dawes, who farmed the land in 1581, was also village constable in 1577-8 (E.R.O. QSR 66/90 and 78/39). The house was extended in the 19th century and had a large cellar, dairy and 20 rooms. In 1827 45-year-old Thomas Pocklington came to the Hall from Kinoulton, Nottinghamshire. He visited three times at a cost of £1 10s., before settling there. His account book (now in the author's possession) dating from 1773-1852 records this.     19. (*lower left*) A view of Vange Hall from the east. In 1886 the owner, Mr. R. L. Curtis employed a builder to remove tiles from the roof and investigate the weird noises that disturbed the inhabitants at night. Swarms of bats were found; but of greater interest was the discovery of two hidden rooms in the roof with boarded floors, nails and hooks for clothes. A register stove downstairs was removed and revealed a large open fireplace with a rough stairway connecting the hidden rooms. These were probably used as hiding places for recusant Catholic priests in Elizabethan times. A corner cupboard that had been used as an altar was also found. An inside stairway was then put up to the rooms and two dormer windows were inserted in the roof (see 18) and the rooms were used for servants (account from the late Mr. A. P. Curtis).     20. (*lower right*) The 500-year-old manor house of North Benfleet which stood near the church and was formerly surrounded by a moat. The manor was held by a branch of the Tyrell family in the 15th and 16th centuries (T. Wright, *The History and Topography of Essex*, 1835). The house was demolished 40 years ago

# IV Farms

Nearly all the farms in the designated area of Basildon have disappeared but the marshes of Goldings and Marsh Farm are still being farmed. The original farmhouse at Goldings Farm was said to have been built by a Dutchman who came to repair the sea-walls in the 17th century (see Nos. 115, 116 & 117). Marsh Farm has an ancient barn which may have belonged to Paprills Farm that stood nearby in the 17th century.

21. Fairhouse Farm, Church Road, Basildon about 1890. The man in the photograph is probably the farmer, Mr. Joseph Moss. The house was demolished in the early 1950s. Fairhouse School is named after the farm which stood on or near the school site. An earlier house stood a little further to the north. Up to the mid-19th-century, Basildon Fair was held in the vicinity on Holy Rood Day, 14 September. It was once of considerable importance but by 1740 it had become a toy fair, although well attended (P. Morant, Vol. I). In 1871, Palin in *Stifford and its Neighbourhood*, stated that there was a meadow called the Fair Field in which 'until comparitively recent time cattle used to be bought and sold'. One of the last people to farm the land here was Mr. Eldred Moss.

2. Hunts Farm, Basildon in 1958. ituated on the south side of Basildon oad, it was destroyed in 1961 when the elds that had grown corn and fed cattle r centuries were cut through by Cranes arm Road and covered by earth tipping. oday, Basildon Road and the farm are overed by the No. 2 Industrial Site. ccording to the Manor Court Rolls of aindon it was called Caves in 1474 Guildhall Library MS.10, 312/131). In 839 the farm was occupied by George lunt who then gave his name to the roperty (Tithe Map, Laindon, E.R.O. /CT 199). As late as 1916 Hunts was ill copyhold property belonging to the lanor of Laindon.

23. (*top left*) Oliphants, Basildon, 1902. Early this century the timber-built Tudor house was destroyed fire. It was rebuilt and in the 1930s became Basildo Rectory. During the 1940s it was destroyed by a bo and again rebuilt. Today the Ford Tractor Plant sta on the site. The family from which it took its name lived in Basildon seven centuries ago. There is ment of Juliana Honeywand in 1249 and Henry de Uniwe in 1254 (P. H. Reaney). In 1484 'Onyfaunts' was he by John Cornwallis of the Prior of St. John of Jerusalem (P. Morant), and in 1570 Thomas Kent le his son the lease of 'Allyvants' (E.R.O. 18 ER 12). There have been many variations on the spelling of the name including 'Elephants'. By a decree of the High Court of Chancery, Oliphants was sold in 1848 for £4,730 to the tenant James Raynham who lived at Botelers, Basildon (P. Benton).

24. (*top right*) Southfields Farm, Dunton. The big Ford Research Centre now covers the site. The hou originally had the date 1710 and the initials *CT* by t south door. Early last century there was old oak wainscotting with several shields of the arms of the Tyrells and in a window were the arms of the Cogge-shale family. The Tyrell arms had been removed fro the Tyrell home, Heron Hall, East Horndon on its demolition in about 1789. Southfields Farm also belonged to the family. In 1837 the tenant Mrs. An Squier paid £105 per annum for 161 acres and land tax of £6 16s. (Sale Catalogue E.R.O. B1234).

25. (*centre left*) Blue House Farm, Laindon, 1959. Blue House Farm Community Centre now stands on the site. As the name suggests the building, dating from the mid-18th century or earlier, was once pair blue (Town and Country Planning List). Deeds of 1851 show that it was once known as Little Gubbin or Gobions (E.R.O. D/D FA E42-12). In 1587 John Crushe left the farm 'upon which I do dwell . . . called by the name of Lytell Gobbins,' to Mary his wife (E.R.O. D/ABW 9/273). A terrier of 1828 give the amount of land as 192 acres with 25 fields with quaint names - Great and Little Madmans, Tory Mea Hoppet and Joy Field (E.R.O. D/DFa E 28).

26. (*above*) The 16th-century barn at Blue House Farm, Laindon in 1959, which was later destroyed by fire in November 1966 (Ministry of Town and Country Planning). In the 17th century there was a windmill which stoc in St. Nicholas Lane with the Little Gobions (Blue House) property. On a deed of 1618 it was stated to have be lately built by John Pake. Robert Payne left it to his son Robert in 1628 but it appears to have disappeared by (E.R.O. D/DFa T 49).

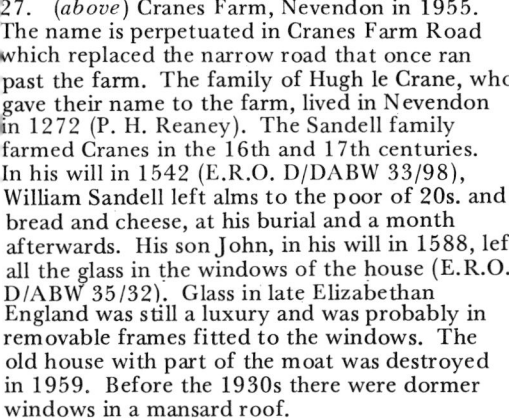

27. (*above*) Cranes Farm, Nevendon in 1955. The name is perpetuated in Cranes Farm Road which replaced the narrow road that once ran past the farm. The family of Hugh le Crane, who gave their name to the farm, lived in Nevendon in 1272 (P. H. Reaney). The Sandell family farmed Cranes in the 16th and 17th centuries. In his will in 1542 (E.R.O. D/DABW 33/98), William Sandell left alms to the poor of 20s. and bread and cheese, at his burial and a month afterwards. His son John, in his will in 1588, left all the glass in the windows of the house (E.R.O. D/ABW 35/32). Glass in late Elizabethan England was still a luxury and was probably in removable frames fitted to the windows. The old house with part of the moat was destroyed in 1959. Before the 1930s there were dormer windows in a mansard roof.

28. (*top right*) Brewitts Farm, Laindon. The red brick farmhouse was dated late 18th and early 19th centuries (R.C.H.M. Vol. IV). The barn which was last used as a cowhouse, dated from the 17th century. The farm was owned in 1839 by John Brewitt (hence the name) and was occupied by Thoroton Pocklington (E.R.O. Tithe Award Map 1839 D/CT 199). Today the site is part of Gloucester Park.

29. (*centre right*) Framptons Farm, Nevendon, 1930. This 16th-century house (R.C.H.M. Vol. IV), stood to the east of the church where the present day sewage works are. William and Thomas Austen, who probably lived here in 1653, are among those who endorsed the indictment of Mary Hurst for witchcraft. She was accused of bewitching William Hodge who was 'wasted and consumed' on 24 May 1653. Happily for Mary she was reprieved (C. L'Estrange Ewen, *Witch-hunting and Witch Trials*).

30. (*bottom right*) Kiln Farm, Pitsea, which stood to the south of the railway line between Pitsea Station and Vange Wharf. Nathaniel Dore, in his will of 1688 left to his 'kinswoman Avis Broughton, Wetherards and Ponders, 50 acres of marsh and uplands at Pitsea' (E.R.O. 185

BR 12). The uplands are now covered by Elm Tree Road, River View, Avondale Road, The Meads and Claremont Drive. The Pitsea Manor Records of 1859 mention 16 acres on this farm on which a lime kiln had recently been built. At that time it was known as Wetherards and Ponders (E.R.O. D Br M78). The house had exposed beams, a dairy and a brick oven. Mr. G. A. Crooks was the last person to farm all the land.

31.   Hill Farm, Vange. This 17th-century farmhouse stood on the hill above Mapleford Sweep (R.C.H.M. Vol. IV). At the side of the central chimney stack was a staircase with a door in it. The earliest recorded mention of the name come from an account of Henry de Birlyngham, serjeant of Barstable, when one acre of uncultivated land on 'le Fangehul' w grazed by the manor sheep in 1345 (P.R.O. SC 6/1245/6). In 1794 a farmer named Peacock paid £40 a year for its 60 acres. The farm then became known as 'Peacocks' (Colby's Map, 1844, Southend Library). In 1832 John Hockley farmed the land, paying £2 14s. poor rate at 1s. in the pound (E.R.O. D/P 298/11). The author's grandfather, Alfred John Moss was the last person to farm the land.

32.   Pitsea Rectory, about 1958. It stood in Rectory Road on the site of St. Gabriel's Church and was originally Shophouse Farm. In 1833 the land was farmed by Daniel Abrey. In 1845 it was owned and occupied by the Rev. L. T. Edwards (E.R.O. Tithe Map D/CT 274) and appears to have been occupied by the rectors of Pitsea from that date until the present rectory was built. For some years this century, however, the rector lived in a nearby bunga-low. Early in the 19th century there was a big fire at Shophouse which destroyed all the farm buildings and the south end of the house. The farm buildings were rebuilt and one of them later became the Church which was replaced by the present building in 1964. The red brick part of the house was the 19th-century building that survived the fire. The house once had a reputation for being haunted.

33.   Luncies Farm, Vange in the 1920s. The house stoo on the north side of Luncies Road. It was one of the firs farms in the district to be sold for building and gipsies camped on its derelict fields for many years. The house was demolished in 1955. The Nevendon Church Registe record that Marrion, wife of Nicholas Hutchine was buri from Luncies in 1658. In 1922-3 two wells on the farm were found to have medicinal properties. The water was widely advertised and sold at about 1s. a pint, in compet ition with the spring water just over Vange boundary (se nos. 120 & 121) until the sanitary authorities analysed a sample and it was found to be unfit for either drinking or domestic use (Southend Standard Jan. 11/18, 1923).

34, 35 & 36. Merricks or Riverside Farm, Vange about 1920. This 16th-century house stood near Vange Wharf and was destroyed by fire in 1961. The farm was known successively as Bigwoods, Merricks, Wharf or Riverside Farm. It apparently took the name Bigwoods from the Bigod family who were related to the Giffords, lords of the manor of Bowers. William Bygod, son of John Bigod of Vange (Vange), was the heir of John Gifford, knight of Bowers, in 1348 (E.R.O. Calendar of Inquisitions Post Mortem). The name of Merricks is probably a corruption of Merrywigs. The farm was associated with the family of John Meryk in 1515 (P. H. Reaney). Originally Merrywigs referred to another farm mentioned in Vange Church Registers in 1602. This probably stood on Merrywigs Marsh where old Vange people used to say the biggest house in the parish once stood. A narrow, sunken lane known as Love Lane, formerly at the west end of Slades, led to the marsh. A memorandum in the church registers concerning which farms should repair the churchyard fence would suggest that Merrywigs may have fallen into decay and Bigwoods on Vange Wharf took over the land and the name (E.R.O. D/P298). Bound in Vange Church Register is a deed of 1691 which relates to Merricks. Fields called Slades and Upper and Lower Bridgewood are mentioned (ibid.). The Slade was to the north of High Road, Vange. Upper Bridgewood (probably a corruption of Bigwood) was a field behind the *Barge* inn. The Moss family were the last farmers of Merricks. A timber yard now covers the site of the farm.

No. 34 shows the farm seen from the sea wall, early this century, with a 16th-century barn on the right and No. 36 shows the fireplace in the dining room.

# V Homes

Apart from the manor houses and farms, the homes of Basildon people last century were mostly small cottages. Many of these had tiny lean-to bedrooms with ceilings sloping down to the floor, referred to by the old Essex folk as 'gander hutches', where children, single lodgers or husbands (if their wives were ill) slept.

37. Basildon Bridge, Vange. The present *Bull* public house stands on the site of the late 17th-century cottages in the centre of the picture. In the background on the right is Fairview Hall where concerts and dances were held in the early years of this century. Note the triangular green with the horse and cart. On the left are the Railway Cottages.

38. Railway Cottages, Bull Road (now Clay Hill Road). They stood approximately at the rear of the present *Bull*, and are thought to have been the 18th-century poor house. Under the new Poor Law of 1834 parishes were grouped together to support a central workhouse which replaced the old parish workhouses. On the Basildon Tithe Map of 1841 the Parish House (old poor house) is shown on a site that corresponds with these cottages (E.R.O. D/CT 22 ). In 1841, 8s. was paid for insurance for the Poor House (E.R.O. D/P 278/5). An old inhabitant told the author's father that the old lath and plaster walls were encased in brick and that afterwards the builder threw the old plaster walls out through the windows. The central chimney stack and ladder-like stairs showed the age of the building. One owner who retired from the *Vange Bells* and came to live here built two rooms on to the west end of the cottages.

39. The old Basildon Rectory in 1960. It replaced an earlier rectory that stood near the entrance to Honey Pot Lane in Pipps Hill Road (now Pipps Hill Close). Built at the expense of the then rector, Rev. John E. Collis, it cost an estimated £7,000 or more. On a marble slab let into the outer wall was an inscription:
' If thou chance to find
A new house to thy mind
Be good to the poor
As God give thee store
Then my money is not lost.'
In the 1930s this house became Rectory Farm and Oliphants in Rectory Road became the residence of the rector.

40. (*above left*) White House in Old Pitsea Village, 1930. It stood almost opposite Rectory Road and dated from the 17th century (Ministry of Town and Country Planning). It was demolished in 1965 to make way for the by-pass. White House had been the home and shop of John Willsmer, the last Pitsea miller and baker. Bread baked on the premises was sold here and at one time it was the only grocer's shop in the village. After 1913 the shop was used by a boot repairer, Mr. Tew. The repairs were done in the old bakehouse and a doctor from Wickford held his surgery in the front room leading out of the shop.

41. (*above right*) The old brick baker's oven in the White House. The bread was made from flour ground in Pitsea Windmill. The photograph was taken in 1964 by the author, when the house was derelict.

42. (*centre*) Telegraph and Wembley Cottages, High Road, Pitsea in 1932. The cottages (opposite Rectory Road) were destroyed in 1965. The Pitsea Court Rolls (held at the E.R.O.) suggest that they were once a house called Goldmans and were part of an original farmhouse. In 1555 Thomas Dowre left his wife his house at Pitsea Street called Goldmans (E.R.O. D/ABW 12/75). In 1896 John Cole had a wheelwrights shop on the premises (deeds at Basildon Corporation Office). Someone on the staff of the *Daily Telegraph* renamed the cottage on the eastern side in 1908. On the walls of Telegraph Cottage (left) was stencilling possibly dating from the 18th century. The leaf pattern was hand-drawn in green, blue and brown in the days before wall paper became universal. The one storey addition (on the right) was a dairy and still-room with stone-flagged floor and bake-oven.

43. (*above*) The Old Parsonage, Pitsea in the 1930s. It stood on the south side of High Road, almost opposite Pitsea School. A typical Essex weather-boarded house, in its last years it was refronted, modernised and extended, retaining the original ceiling beams in the kitchen. A secret hiding place or priest's hole was found in a bedroom. At one time there was part of a moat to the south and west of the house. The church registers record the burial of Hannah, wife of John Melbank from Pitsea Parsonage in 1742. By the 1930s the house had not been inhabited by Pitsea parsons for at least a century.

44. Peartree Cottages, Pitsea, in 1936. Standing to the south of High Road and to the east of Aversley Road, the cottages backed on to Poor House Field and were probably at one time the poor house. In Pitsea parish accounts an entry for 23 November 1843, states that at a vestry held that day, it was agreed by the churchwardens and overseers to surrender the ground hired of the ladies of the manor 'for the purpose of erecting a cottage or tenements for the use of the poor at a rental of 5s. per annum'. In 1837, 8s. insurance had been paid for the poor house (E.R.O. D/P 182).

45. Old thatched cottage, High Road, Vange, which stood on the north side of the road near the top of Paynters Hill.

46. Black Cottages, High Road, Vange in 1936. They stood opposite the small Catholic Church near Barge Corner. This kind of cottage was often built on land stolen from the road. A doctor held his surgery in the cottage on the right in which old Mrs. English lived.

47. Vange Rectory, 1930s, the site is now covered by Vange Zoo. The Rector, Rev. J. A. Stewart moved here when it was first built in 1836. At that time it was considered to be a very fine house as the old rectory (to the right of the entrance to the old churchyard) was only a small timber house. Timbers from this building were used to build the two cottages still standing today at the top of Paynters Hill. Trees and shrubs planted in 1836 are still to be seen in the zoo grounds. Examples of the prices paid are: red cedar 9d., two mountain ash 4d. Dating from the same period is an interesting bill for the rector's groceries from Romford. 1lb of coffee cost 2s., 2lb of sugar 1s., 2lb of raisins and 1oz of lemon peel ½d (E.R.O. D/DOP 839/93/1-2).

48. Old cottages that stood to the east of the *Five Bells*, Vange. Note the lean-to bedrooms. The site is now covered by the roundabout.

49. Vange Hall Cottages, standing the east of Vange Primary School in High Road, Vange. They are exam of late Victorian architecture, built R. L. Curtis in 1883 for workers in brickfield which he established on marsh by Marsh Farm.

# VI  Old Parish Churches

The Parish Churches of the Basildon area have considerable medieval work in their fabric. Perhaps the oldest church is All Saints', Vange, parts of which date back to the late 11th century. The nave is late 11th or 12th century and the great chancel arch is 3 feet 10 inches thick. The church may have been built on the orders of Ralph, son of Turold who held the manor at the time of the Domesday Survey. The 15th-century rood loft staircase can still be seen.

The nave of St. Nicholas, Laindon, is 800 years old and the chancel and south aisle were added in the 14th century. The timber roof is 500 years old and the bell turret rests on an arched frame of timber that once grew in the nearby woods. The 17th century or earlier timber building at the west end known as the Priest's House may have replaced the home of the chantry priest who served in the chantry in the south aisle, endowed by Thomas de Berdefeild in 1329. Both St. Nicholas and Holy Cross, Basildon, have similar 15th-century carvings on their porches. The oldest part of Holy Cross is the 14th-century nave. The chancel was rebuilt in 1597 by the rector, Arthur Denham. The weather vane has the initials and date F.A.1702. The initials stand for Francis Aylett who was responsible for the restoration in 1702 and lived at the Tudor house known as Oliphants.

St. Michael's, Pitsea, except for the tower, was rebuilt in 1871 at a total cost of £1,288 10s. 10d., of which £1,264 12s. 3d. was raised by public subscription. Of this the patrons gave over £1,000 and the rector £100. The architect was Sir Arthur Blomfield. The embattled tower with gargoyles was built in the 16th century and on its east doorway are masons' marks.

At the bottom of the steep hill at Langdon Hills stands the former church of St. Mary the Virgin and All Saints', now a private residence. It stands on the site of an earlier church and was restored and added to in the 17th century. In 1877 St. Mary's church was built at the top of the hill and the old church ceased to be used except for burials.

At Nevendon, St. Peter's church still possesses the original lancet windows. In his history of the church, the Rev. A. W. Hands wrote that the existing walls of the chancel are 13th century, a relic of the building erected by a member of the Fitz Lewis family as a chantry chapel to serve some hunting lodge of the family.

Bowers Gifford church was probably built by the Gifford family in the 14th century. It was rebuilt in the 16th century but there is 14th-century work in the south wall and tower. Dunton church has 500-years-old timbers supporting the belfry and there is 13th-century work in North Benfleet church.

0. (*opposite*) The church of Holy Cross, Basildon about the turn of the century, showing the west tower dating from 1500.

1. (*above*) Another view of Holy Cross Church. In 1230, Geoffrey de Bartlesden (Basildon) and Idonea, his wife quitclaimed the advowson of this church, referred to as 'the church of Bartlesdon', to the Bishop of London and his church of St. Paul (E.A.S.T. Vol. XVI NS p. 278). The Bishop was also patron of Laindon Parish and one rector served the two parishes until the formation of the United Parish of Basildon. In his will of 10 March 1348-9, Robert Travers devised to the church of Holy Cross in Basildon, Sir William Say, Rector of Basildon and his successors, the annual rent of 78s. 6d. paid by Richard Noblepas and 'all his brood' for lands and tenements held in bondage in Basildon and Nevendon for celebrating Masses every Saturday at the altar of St. Mary, for the souls of his father and his ancestors and for the health of Joan, Robert's mother, himself and his wife, Eleanor, while they should live and for their souls 'when they departed the world of flesh' and 'one candle of one and a half pounds of wax' was to be burnt before the sepulchre of our Lord from Good Friday until second Vespers and one torch worth 18d. to be kept in the church for lighting daily at the raising of the Body of Our Lord' (E.R.O. D/DHf 41/40).

52. (*top left*) St. Nicholas Church, Laindon, surrounded by unspoilt countryside at the turn of the century.

53. (*above*) Langdon Hills, (old church) 1927. In 1579 the servants of the rector, John Goldring, put his sheep in the church for two days to protect them from the great snow storm which occurred a little after Candlemas, 2 February. For this he was ordered by the Archdeacon's Court to pay 6d. to the poor (Archdeaconry of Essex transcripts). In 1 Goldring was said to be a 'drunkard and a quarreler' (E.R.O. 2 S.R. 94/16).

54. (*above right*) Langdon Hills, old church, interior in the 1930s. The picture was taken from the musicians' galler where the villagers used to make their own music with flutes, oboes and other instruments. It shows the Royal Arms Charles II which were put up at the Restoration. The framing filled with plaster on which the arms were painted rep the figures which stood on the rood beam before the Reformation:- Our Lord, St. Mary and St. John. Below can be the name of the Churchwarden of the time, John Elliett, and an inscription from Proverbs (24. 21.). The church wa enlarged in 1834 and arches were opened on the north side and a building, 17ft. by 23ft. was added. The pulpit and entrance doors were renewed at this time and the Creed and Lord's Prayer were put up in the Chancel. (Information from Parish Books in custody of Rector.)

An old picture of North Benfleet
[ch]urch, taken before 1903 when the west
[to]wer was built. The sturdy timbers of the
[15]th-century bell turret still remain.

5. St. Michael's Church, Pitsea,
[su]rrounded by elm trees, c. 1900.
[sc]enes connected with the church can
[b]e reconstructed from old documents.
[In] 1543 the villagers saw their priest,
[R]ichard Gray, buried in the churchyard,
[be]tween the churchyard cross and the
[ch]ancel door. He left alms—beer, bread
[an]d cheese for the poor folk who came to
[pr]ay for him and 'every pore body' was
[to] receive 1d. and women with child
[2d]. (E.R.O. D/ABW 16). In 1589 the
[co]ngregation saw Margaret Paine stand
[in] the church to do penance for
[im]morality. She also had to do public
[pe]nance in Billericay market (E.R.O.
[Ar]chdeaconry of Essex transcripts).

7. Westley Hall, Langdon Hills, 1955,
[st]anding on or near the site of a lost
[p]arish church. 500 years ago Westley was
[a] separate parish belonging to the Dean
[an]d Chapter of St. Pauls. When in 1297,
[th]e Dean visited the church he found it
[in] ruinous condition. Cattle were feed-
[in]g in the churchyard as the fence was
[b]roken. The wooden font leaked, the
[n]ave windows were unglazed and there
[w]as no bell. The revenue was too small
[to] support a resident priest and by 1432
[n]o one would accept the benefice because
[o]f this. The patrons besought the Bishop
[to] amalgamate it with Langdon Hills and
[sa]nction was given in July 1432. The
[re]ctor of Langdon Hills had to celebrate
[M]ass there annually on the feast of its
[d]edication. However, the church soon
[fe]ll into decay and the exact place where
[it] stood is unknown. The ancient barn
[is] said to contain timbers from the church
[(]V.C.H. Essex Vol.II).

58. (*above left*) Vange Church in the 19[_] or earlier. Some of the elm trees may ha[_] been those, or their immediate successors[_] mentioned by the Archdeacon of Essex w[_] he visited the churchyard between Augus[_] 1815 and June 1817. He found 11 pollar[_] elms, 11 elms and one ash (*Essex Review* Vol. XXII No. 86). In 1503 the body of [_] Sawnder was carried up the church path f[_] burial; driven before the coffin was a shee[_] value 13d. This was a medieval Essex cus[_] 'the fordrive', an offering of animals to th[_] church on one's death, which was driven before the funeral procession (E.R.O. 20 [_] 2).

59. (*above*) This photograph of All Sain[_] Church, Vange is probably pre-1914. The[_] railings, surrounding the graves of the Pocklington family, who farmed Vange H[_] in the 19th century, were removed during Second World War.

60. (*above*) All Saints' Church, Vange, 1896. This was before the restoration which converted it 'from a whitewashed barn into the prettiest church in the neighbourhood' according to a contemporary news report. Notice the old box pews which kept out drafts and prevented dogs, which were allowed in church with their owners, from roaming around. On either side of the west window are tablets with the Creed and Ten Commandments. Candles are used for lighting.

61. (*right*) Vange Church about 1920. There were now oil lamps and a different coal burning stove.

# VII Schools

The first school in Basildon was founded in 1617 by farmer John Puckle who remembered the less fortunate children of Laindon and Basildon in his will. A wooden tablet in St. Nicholas' church, Laindon records that he left in trust all his lands to maintain a schoolmaster for teaching a competent number of poor children. The endowment was Puckle's Farm, 62½ acres in Wash Road, Laindon. (V.C.H.) The 17th-century farmhouse was demolished early this century. In 1876, a Board School was built in Laindon, this is now Laindon Park School.

Few adults in Vange could read or write in 1839, according to a Diocesan Return about provision of education for the poor. There was only a Sunday School where 18 boys and 12 girls were taught in the church. A seraphine (wood instrument with keyboard, wind chest and bellows) accompanied the singing. This Sunday School was in union with the National Society and had been in existence about ten years. It was managed and supervised by the rector assisted by a master. The annual expenditure was about £3 and the annual receipts £2 10s. The scholars, some of whom came from Basildon received their education freely. There were few subscriptions, the rest being made up by the rector. Funds were difficult to procure; the rector stated that a 'narrow and grudging spirit prevailed in the parish' (E.R.O. D/B30/28/19).

Nevendon had an elementary school in the 18th century. A tombstone in the churchyard records that Elizabeth Kirkham, who died in 1788, was mistress of a school for 27 years. In the 19th century a cowman's wife kept a school in a cottage in the narrow lane that led to Basildon, now replaced by Crane's Farm Road. At a later date a school met in a thatched cottage that stood opposite the turning to Burnt Mills Road. The teacher, Mrs. Atkins could only make her mark in the church register when she was married, so she is not likely to have taught writing (*The Parish Church of Nevendon*, Rev. A. W. Hands, 1925).

In 1807, Pitsea had no school of any kind (E.R.O. D/AEM2/4 1807). In the 19th century there was a dame school at Bull Farm (now two cottages). In 1949 the late Mrs. Upson told the author that she remembered attending the school and sitting on the lower step of the stairs reading her lessons. A Mrs. Large ran the school with her daughter Annie and Miss Bell, her neice.

In the Diocesan Return of 1839 it was stated that Langdon Hills only had a Sunday School which had been established for 6½ years. (E.R.O. D/P 20/28/18.) No charges were made for this schooling and few were without any education at all. The Sunday School was held in a schoolroom that had been built on the north-west side of the old church in 1834. The north door in the church (which is now a private house) led into this room, long since demolished. About twenty children were educated in Dame Schools; a few attended a little school in Laindon, but the farmers required the children to work in the fields at a very early age.

62. St. Nicholas Church, Laindon about 1890. Note the 17th-century, or earlier, timber annexe at the west end kn
as the Priest's House (R.C.H.M. Vol. IV). About 1837 this annexe housed Puckle's School where 20 boys and girls w
taught reading, writing and arithmetic, free of charge. There were some children who paid at the rate of 4d. or 8d. p
week according to the instruction given. The last schoolmaster, James Hornsby, who taught there for 48 years was q
remarkable. He was born in 1800, without the lower part of his left arm and before his appointment as schoolmaste
worked as a horseman on a farm and could plough and do all farm work. He was also parish clerk and sexton (E.A.S.
NS Vol. XVIII p. 76-7). In 1855, his second wife, Mrs. Catherine Hornsby, taught the girls sewing (Kelly's *Directory*

64. An old picture of the interior of St. Nicholas, Laindon, showing the huge beams in the belfry. James Hornsby, reputed to be a capable teacher and a strict disciplinarian used to tie naughty boys to one of these beams. He also used the cane. The Hornsbys lived in the Priest's House as well as keeping school there. Six farmers' sons from Basildon were weekly boarders, sleeping in the attic which had no window, only a glass tile. The last Mrs. Hornsby used to hang her washing to dry in the church during damp weather. When a woman visitor protested at this, she replied, 'Well people don't go to church on Toosdays', Pots and pans were also kept in the church and the Hornsbys' sheep grazed in the churchyard (E.A.S.T. NS Vol. XVIII p. 76). The author's grandfather stayed with the Hornsbys as a boy and remembered going up to bed and looking into the belfry through a hole in the wall.

63. The graves of James Hornsby and his three wives outside the Priest's House. The damp and draughty schoolhouse may have contributed to the deaths of his wives. Sarah died in August 1851, Catherine in February 1859 and Catherine II in March 1883. Hornsby himself lived to the age of 83 and died in May 1887.

65. (*above*) The old Nevendon School, demolished in March 1972. The photograph was taken in 1955 when it was a private house. It stood to the west of St. Peter's Church, Nevendon and was built in 1886 as a National School. Before this the Rev. W. M. Kerr had opened a school in the tithe barn ( Rev. A. W. Hands, *The Parish Church of Nevendon, Essex*, 1925).

66. (*above right*) This cottage, formerly the village school, stands near the church of St. Mary, Langdon Hills. It lost its thatched roof in 1962. J. Cockfield Dimsdale gave the site for the school, which was a piece of waste ground on the roadside and in 1860 the school was built at a cost of £200. It consisted of a schoolroom and accommodation for the schoolmistress. It was enlarged at a cost of £50 in 1880. A stone with the inscription 'L. H. S. 1880 WB' dates from this time and records the name of the builder, William Boardman. In 1894 about 35 children attended the school, ranging in age from four to 12 years old. The master received £30 per annum and half the government grant, which in 1881 was £48. He did not live at the school because the accommodation was too poor (E.R.O. T/P 89). The school was under the National Society until 1903 when it was recognised as a Church of England School. In 1907 a parish meeting decided to have a new Council School as the old school was too small, and on 13 February 1911, the new school (now Langdon Hills Primary) was opened. (Notes from the Rector of Langdon Hills, Rev. E. C. Telford, 1959).

67. (*opposite below*) Bowers Gifford school group, *c.* 1899. In the second row (third from left), is a dwarf teacher, she is standing on a form next to Emily Talbot who lived at Tarpots Farm. The girl with long curls (fifth from left in the second row), is May Eaton whose father was Station Master at Pitsea for many years. Second from the left in the back row is Ada Cue; her mother, the headmistress, is standing at the end of the row. She used to say 'I'll box your years' and pronounced fatigue 'fattygue'. The photograph and information came from Mrs. B. M. Deacon (fourth from the right, in the second row). Note the boys' hob nail boots. The school was originally a National School and the buildings were built in 1846. There was an average attendance of 56 and Kelly's *Directory* for 1890 gives Mrs. Mary Ann Cue as mistress of the school. The building still stands on the High Road near the *Prohibition,* and a new school was built near the rectory in 1936.

68. (*above*) Pitsea school group, about the time of the First World War, or shortly after. From 1846 to about 1908 Pitsea children had attended the school at Bowers Gifford. In 1911 a Council School was built for 264 children. Just before this there was a temporary building in a field by the side of Church Hill Path, not far from the High Road. This school site is now covered by the fly-over.

69. (*above*) The old school-house and school, Vange in 1930. This still stands by Vange Zoo, although completely modernised. The small one-storey building on the right was the schoolroom and the headmistress lived in the cotta next to it, until after the turn of the century, although a new schoo had been built in 1876 (now Vang Primary School). This, the first school in Vange had been built *c.* 1858, when the Rev. E. Sendall received a grant of land from Sir Charles Smith, lord of the manor and patron, to build a school and two cottages (Vange Parish Books

70. School group, Vange, showing group IV, Standard I, in about 1911. Note the girls' white pinafores.

# VIII Roads

Many of the roads and lanes in and around Basildon are very ancient. In the medieval manorial rolls references are found to roads which carry the same names today. Barking Abbey in Essex held Hawkesbury (Bush) manor in Fobbing within the New Town boundary. Manor courts held there in 1455 and 1459 mention a ditch overflowing in 'Dreystret' (Dry Street) (E.R.O. D/Dsg M3). Noak Hill Road appears to have been known as North Street in 1474 (Laindon Court Rolls at Guildhall Library MS 10, 312/243).

At a manor court at Laindon in 1374 an inquest was held to consider if a road made across the lord's land called 'Schotelond' and then to his field called 'Joynhale' and 'Joynalemade' was known as a common cart way without the lord's permission. It was said it could be used by 'strangers in pilgrimage to Canterbury riding on horseback or going on foot' (Laindon Court Rolls, Guildhall Library, MS 10, 312/125). A field known as Joiners Hill on the south corner of St. Nicholas Lane at the entrance from High Road is shown on the 1839 Laindon Tithe Map (E.R.O. DCT 199). This might have been the Joynhale mentioned in the court roll and suggests that St. Nicholas Lane was once a pilgrims' way.

Bridges over streams (now piped and unnoticed by the present day motorist) caused much trouble and annoyance to Basildon travellers in medieval days. In 1374 a bridge called 'le Personesbregge' (Parsons Bridge) was in ruins owing to the negligence of the Rector of Laindon who was responsible for its upkeep (Laindon Court Rolls, Guildhall Library, MS 10, 312/125). This bridge was on the Basildon Road which is now covered by the No. 2 Industrial Site. Bequests were often made in wills of money for the repair of roads. Agnes Kent of Vange in 1552 left 6s. 8d. to mend two 'slowes' (sloughs) which were soft muddy patches or holes in the road (E.R.O. D/DABW 22/56).

Encroachments on the road became another problem. In 1618 William Wiseman encroached on the highway leading from Laindon Cross towards Dunton Waylett, and he allowed trees to overhang the highway from Laindon Cross towards Horndon (E.R.O. Q.S. Bundle 4/1). From this it would appear that Laindon Cross was probably the place where Noak Hill Road, Wash Road, Dunton Road and Laindon High Road crossed before the re-alignment of Noak Hill Road. Clement Dawes of Vange Hall in 1581 took away part of the highway leading from Vange to Chelmsford and from Vange to Billericay (E.R.O. QSR 78/39).

In addition to the difficulty of travelling over bad roads in the 18th and 19th centuries, thieves abounded and farmers coming home from market would travel in bands as an added security against robbery. An 1815 newspaper gives an account of the robbery of two Laindon men on their way home from Romford market. As they rode in a chaise they were stopped by three footpads armed with bludgeons who took money, a watch and a yard of scotch cambric from them (E.R.O. T/P110/35).

71. A view of the Basildon of yesterday. junction of Rectory Road and Gardiner's with the old Basildon post office in the fo ground. The lane took its name from the Gardiner family who farmed Wasketts Fa for 90 years until 1962. It was known in as 'Dryvers Lane leading from Waskettes to the end of the same lane towards Basil (E.R.O. QSR 149/39).

72. Church Road, Basildon at the approach to Clay Hill Road, known as Bull Road in 1932. There are now shops on the right and Swan Mead School to the left. This stretch of road was narrow, lonely and shaded by tall elm trees, dark at night. It was reputedly haunted by a mischievous ghost that threw people over the hedge into the fields. One of those who complained of this treatment was the tenant of Basildon Hall. Men leaving the *Bull* at night would not walk home alone but would wait for friends to accompany them. The author's father was apparently unaware of this legend but as a boy was always afraid of this part of the road.

73. Honey Pot Lane. This photograph, taken in the 19 by the author, shows the former entrance to the lane fr Pipps Hill Road near the present Pipps Hill Close. On Chapman and Andre's Map, 1777 it is shown as running from Clay Hill to Pipps Hill. In winter it was almost im able owing to the soft, sticky, yellow 'London Clay' wh gave it the distinctive name of Honey Pot. In 1906 it w described as a particularly lonely place with not half a d houses within a radius of three miles, a narrow deep-rut road leading to distant farms. (From an account of the murder of Mr. and Mrs. Watson, Southend Library, Petr Newscuttings 1.029.3 Ess.) Now the busy town centre stands on part of its old track, the original line of which was until recently marked by a line of old elm trees by Southernhay.

4. High Road, Bowers Gifford about 1906. The photograph was taken near the site of the present Basildon Corporation Offices, looking towards the *Gun*. In 1712 this particular part of the road was said to be 'broken, dangerous and out of repair' (E.R.O. QSR 553/6).

5. The Wash, Wash Road, Laindon in the 1930s. At a manor court in 1443, Thomas Bone was told to scour (clean) a ditch at Seynt Mary Way (Laindon Court Rolls, Guildhall Library MS 10 312/127) and a map of 1593 identifies St. Mary Way as Wash Road (E.R.O. DD/P/P3A).

76. The Old Basildon Road, Laindon, a winding country lane now engulfed by the No. 2 Industrial Site.

77. (below) Lee Chapel Lane, formerly Oxford Street, Langdon Hills. Green Lane which joined Oxford Street was, according to tradition, used by Canterbury pilgrims.

78. High Road, Laindon, early this century. Note the poor condition of the road.

79.  Timberlog Lane, Nevendon about the 1920s. In 1667 there was mention of Timberlogg Lane (E.R.O. QSR 412/39). The name probably derives from its use as a route for the timber going towards Vange Wharf. The ancient farm of Mopsies formerly stood to the left of the picture and one of the thatched farm buildings was still standing in the 1930s. In 1965 this section of the lane became the cul-de-sac Timberlog Close.

80.  Pitsea High Road, looking towards Vange, early this century. The entrance to Brickhouse Farm is on the right. The railway bridge in the background was so narrow that it was dangerous when motor transport developed.

81.  High Road, Pitsea in 1932, from the east of the Working Mens' Club looking towards the railway bridge. Behind the wych elms (shading the south side of the road) were the fields of Kiln Farm, owned by Mr. G. A. Crooks who lived in the Old Parsonage further down the road. The Pitsea/Vange boundary crossed the road near here. According to Carey's 'New Itinerary' in 1828, the London to Southend stage coach ran through Vange and Pitsea and there are references to the coach road in Pitsea in the parish accounts for 1805 and 1810 (E.R.O. D/P 182/21).

82. High Road, Pitsea, at the Rectory Road junction looking towards Vange, 1910. Note the road surface and on the left the geese at the roadside.

83. The corn has just been cut in this field on the south side of Pitsea High Road in 1930. The market car park and fly-over now occupy the site.

84. Northlands Drive, Pitsea, situated at the side of the present *Railway Hotel* and leading to Northlands Farm. The name probably derives from the fact that it was the approach road to the north part of Pitsea Hall Manor.

85. Station Lane, Pitsea, early this century. The house on the left was the principal newsagents. When the station was built the question of access had to be considered and the bridlepath leading to the Hall grounds was extended. Previously kept in repair by the Parish, the Railway Company eventually agreed to take over the upkeep. Oxley Parker, negotiating for the landowners, agreed to fence it, planting quick or thorn (The Oxley Parker Papers, Lt.-Col. J. Oxley Parker, D.L., M.A.,). However, the Company soon demurred at the cost in view of the small amount of traffic, threatening to close the station or remove it elsewhere. The road was neglected and it was in such a bad state of repair that the Parish attempted to take over the upkeep at a meeting in 1858. This attempt failed, and for a century, until the Essex County Council took it over, the road remained in a bad condition with mud and pot holes. (From letters re building of Pitsea Station, lent to the author by Mr. E. Pettit.)

Rectory Road Pitsea, looking North.

86.  Rectory Road, Pitsea, looking north. The road continued through the fields of Chalvedon Hall. The state of the roads in 19th-century Essex was very bad and Rectory Road was no exception. The cart wheels made ruts as they sank into the mud. In 1809, £1 17s. 6d. was paid for stubbing the quarters (ridges between the horse track and wheel tracks) down from Pitsea Mill Gate, immediately north of Howard Crescent, to the end of the parish towards Burnt Mills. In 1810 a man and a boy received 16s. for stubbing in ruts on Pitsea roads (E.R.O. D/P 182).

87.  Smiths Lane, latterly known as Briscoe Road, Pitsea. The author remembers this as a narrow lane without houses, running from the west side of Rectory Road. According to tradition it was used by the military and nobility coming from London via Ilford, Romford, Crays Hill and Basildon to Hadleigh Castle. A grant of 1342-3 mentions 'le Smythes Strate' leading from Nevendon towards Depegate Cross as far as Laindon (E.R.O. T/41 29). In a presentment of 1645 it was stated that 'a lane commonly called Smythes Laine' was to be repaired by the inhabitants of Pitsea (E.R.O. QSR 326/38). The Rectory Road end of this old road is now part of the new development in the vicinity of Ashlyns. The rest has been replaced by new housing and Northlands Park.

88. High Road, Vange, by All Saints Church and opposite the present day zoo. This photograph, taken in 1895 shows the tithe barn and other farm buildings belonging to Vange Rectory.

89. Wharf Lane, Vange, about the 1920s. This lane on the east side of High Road, just past the *Barge* inn, is now built over. It led to Vange Wharf, Merricks and Goldings Farms and the marsh farm known as Wick Farm. An old map of Merricks Farm, dated 1754 (E.R.O. D/D sd p. 2) shows the lane as an enclosure called the Hay. Hay means a hedge or enclosure and this was part of the eastern boundary of Merricks Farm. Until 1914 the brickfield owned by Messrs Clarke, Nickolls and Coombs Ltd was situated to the west of the lane.

90. View of Vange Wharf Lane in the 1930s. The lower half
the lane is shown with the railway line and the crossing keeper
little hut in the distance. When the author's parents were
married they were kept in their horse-drawn cab and pelted
with rice before the crossing keeper opened the gates.

91. Basildon Corner, Vange, the present day junction of Clay Hill Road with Church Road, Basildon. The field on the
left of the picture, which is now the site of Perry Springs, Collingwood Terrace and Collingwood Road, was known as
Undermines, a name that goes back to 1602 (E.R.O. D/P 298).

# IX Shops

In 1848 there were only four widely-scattered shops in the Basildon area and therefore window shopping would have been an impossibility. Pitsea could boast one shop and a bakery, but Vange had no shop at all. Christopher Banks was a shopkeeper and smith at Laindon, and Nevendon's shop was at the *Bell* beerhouse (White's *Gazetteer*). Kelly's *Post Office Directory* gives miscellaneous pieces of information about shopkeepers. In 1855 John Tyler, shopkeeper, is mentioned in Basildon. William Mager kept a shop at Vange and William Austin made boots and shoes. George Bettis of Pitsea was a shopkeeper and carrier (Kelly's, E.R.O. 1855).

In 1890, W. R. Jackson kept a drapery and grocery shop at Pitsea, no doubt the predecessor of Cook's Stores (nos. 93, 94). There was no post office at Pitsea, and letters were despatched through Bowers Gifford. Laindon had a post office and James Mead kept a shop at the *Prince of Wales*. There was also a shop at Vange (Kelly's, E.R.O. 1890).

92. Inflator House, High Road, Vange before the 1914 war. It stood to the north of the road almost opposite Ramsay Drive. In 1890 it was the village post office and only shop (Kelly's *Directory*, 1890). Mrs Susannah Phillips was the postmistress. When this picture was taken the post office had been moved further east along the road and the shop was kept by Mr. Roberts (outside the shop) and Miss Messer, who was also a dressmaker. It was a popular house of call for the large number of people who cycled from London to Southend during the summer. A huge kettle was always boiling on the open kitchen range and inside the shop a large number of aspidistras flourished.

93. Cook's Shop, High Road, Pitsea in 1898. It stood on the south side of the High Road, east of the market car park and has since disappeared. A row of timber cottages, Bedlam Row, occupied the site 120 years ago. Mr. H. J. Cook opened the first post and telegraph office here in 1897. It was the nearest telegraph office for Vange, Bowers Gifford and parts of Nevendon and Basildon. In the picture, *left to right*, are Miss Cook (H. J. Cook's sister), Fred Wooltorton, Neddie Rayner (postman who had fought in the Crimea), H. J. Cook, Mr. Sheldrake (Mr. Cook's predecessor), Ashley Reddington, H. J. Cook's brother, Mrs. Cook senior, Mrs. Sheldrake, unknown girl. The business closed down in 1964.

94. Cook's Drapery Store and post office at Pitsea, early this century. Note the telegraph boy standing outside the shop. Cook's was the chief drapery store in the area. If you could not get what you required there, the only alternative was to go to Southend.

95. The old thatched post office on Crown Hill, Langdon Hills.

96. The old Bowers Gifford post office. Mr. E. M. Reddington was the postmaster. The photograph was taken about 1920. The old *Gun* inn can be seen in the far distance.

Gales Stores, Vange.

97. Gale's Stores, Vange, demolished in July, 19
The shop stood on the south side of Bull Road (n
Clay Hill Road), at its junction with Timberlog L
and looked out onto Basildon Bridge and the lane
Gale's Corner was a well-known landmark and bu
stop.

98. Miss Annie Weeks standing at the entrance to the fish and greengrocery shop on the south side of Vange High Road, near Kent View Road. Her mother and father are also standing outside the shop. The horse and cart probably belonged to Mr. Weeks.

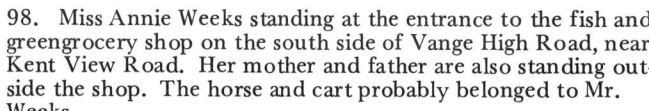

High Street, Vange.

99. Fuller's Drapery Store, High Road, Vange. C
corner of Kent View Road, it had at one time been
post office. Just visible behind the two shops is th
gable of Bartlett's Grocery Store which was appro
by a flight of steps.

# X Inns

Each parish in the designated area of Basildon New Town had at least one inn. Today these have either been rebuilt or had the licence removed to a new house. Only the *Five Bells*, Vange (the oldest); the *Barge*, Vange, and the *Crown*, Langdon Hills have escaped this.

There is a particularly interesting story connected with the *Gun*, Bowers Gifford. In the early 19th century, a Rayleigh miller, with his pockets full of money, stopped there for refreshment. He became suspicious that some men who had left the inn previously intended to harm him. Having a presentment that if he went over Bread and Cheese Hill he would meet his death, he travelled through Rush Bottom Lane by Tarpots and round by Thundersley Church. This action saved his life for the men were lying in wait on the hill with a grave dug ready for him in Thundersley Woods (Benton, *History of Rochford Hundred*, p. 70).

0. *Pitsea Bull* in the latter years of the 19th century. (Drawn by the author from a painting in the possession of the ~~te~~ G. A. Crooks.) The *Prohibition* now stands on the site of this old timber house in High Road, Pitsea. There was a ~~on~~d on the site of the present day car park. The Pitsea Church Registers of 1740 mention the *Bull* or *Green Man*, an ~~i~~dication that the sign may have changed. In 1741 Mary Saunders was buried from 'ye *Green Man*'. John Burrell was ~~th~~e landlord in 1769 (Alehouse Recognizance List, E.R.O. Q/RLV 24/82).

Bull Inn, Vange.

101. The *Bull*, Basildon, soon after it w
rebuilt early this century. Before that i
was a little beer house in one of three s
cottages. The old *Bull* was demolished
1961 and was replaced by the present h
which stands approximately 50 yards to
east of the old inn. The Basildon Churc
Registers record that Joseph, son of Jam
and Martha Arser of Basildon *Bull*, was
baptised in April 1777. In 1778 James
Arser died. Another landlord, John San
ford suffered three bereavements in less
than a year. His 13-year-old son was bu
in September 1793. In November that
another son was born and died nine day
later and in January 1794 his 40-year-o
wife was buried (E.R.O. D/P 278/1).

102. The *Gun* inn, Bowers Gifford in the 1920s. The first recorded landlord was William Butler in
1769 (A.R.L., E.R.O. Q/RLV 24/28). It belonged to the Spitty family and when the estate was sold
in 1917 it was described in the sale catalogue as 'built of brick and slated containing on the ground
floor, bar, bar parlour, dining room, tap room, kitchen, larder, tea room and small spirit store. On
the first floor bagatelle room and four bedrooms. On the second floor, three good attics. In the
basement is a large dry cellar, also buildings and land attached. Rent £75 per annum, let to Luker
and Co. Ltd.' (A copy of the sale catalogue is at Cater Museum, Billericay.) The inn was rebuilt
before the Second World War. In the late 1950s the late Mrs. Upson told the author that 100 years
before, the inn was kept by her father, Charles Henry Ellison, the blacksmith and probably the last
village constable of Bowers. Outside the inn was a huge iron cage in which drunks were put 'to cool
them off'. The stocks stood opposite the inn.

103. The *Prince of Wales* in Wash Road, Laindon, 1931. This was a 17th-century house which was rebuilt in the 1930s (R.C.H.M. Vol. IV). James Mead kept a shop here in 1890 (Kelly's *Directory*, 1890).

104. The *Laindon* Hotel, about 1914, built in 1896 for £3,310 and designed by the architect T.T. Matthews of London. It was to be built by a syndicate in connection with a proposed racecourse. This was to be built at Laindon within 200 yards of the station on Great Buggins and Whelps Farm. It was to be an oval course, 1¾ miles in circumference and the grandstand was to be a replica of the stand at Sandown Park, with accommodation for 2,000 people. However, the scheme never came to fruition (Southend Library, Petre Newscuttings, 1.029.3 Ess).

105. The *Old Fortune of War*. It is said to have been founded by a soldier returning from the Napoleonic Wars. In 1907, R. A. Beckett wrote in *Romantic Essex* that 'although the house has in recent years been rebuilt, it is an old place'. When he visited it 'festivities were going on in a field hard by' and he was told that this was 'Fortune Fair, a yearly event since time immemorial'. Beckett added, 'that like many of these old pleasure fairs, it had shrunk to very small dimensions'. The licence was removed to the present public house in 1928. It is now the printers at the junction of Noak Hill Road and Laindon High Road.

106. The *Crown* Hotel, Langdon in 1908. It has stood on the hill f- over 200 years. In the 18th centu- vestry meetings were often adjour- here. The landlady in 1769 was E- beth Smith (A.R.L., E.R.O. Q/RL 24/82). The plastered sign on the upper storey shows the Imperial C- of State, dated 1874. At the turn the century it was a particularly b- house. Sir Joseph Dimsdale (later Mayor of London) stayed here wh- Goldsmiths was being enlarged. W- he found that his friends staying a- the *Crown* for the hunting and sho- ing were causing the landlord and - family to give up their beds he per- suaded the brewers to enlarge the - Workmen building the new church labourers laying the railway line in also stayed at the inn. An argume- ative labourer was horsewhipped b- the landlady on one occasion. On another occasion gipsies camping i- the district, broke into the larder a- stole all the food. (Information fr- the granddaughter of the proprieto- at that time Mrs. Hannah Raynor.)

107. The *Harrows* inn, North Benfleet in 1910, drawn by the author from a painting in the possession of the late Mr. J. Reeks. It stood just outside the New Town boundary in Harrow Road and was about 250 years old. In 1769 the lan- lord was Thomas Sharpe (A.R.L., E.R.O. Q/RLV 24). The North Benfleet manor rolls record that in 1785 Harrow Ro- was called Almshouse Lane and the rent of the inn was 2s. per annum (E.R.O. D/Dwt M 25). The landlord in 1790 wa- James Sharpe (A.R.L., E.R.O. Q/RLV 44), and in 1803, John Dennis (A.R.L., E.R.O. Q/RLV 57).

108. The ruins of the *Harrows*, North Benfleet, after a fire in July 1914. Villagers lost possessions in the blaze as cutlery and other articles had been taken to the inn in preparation for the Harvest Supper. Business appears to have been carried on in the shed and tent alongside the ruins. The inn was rebuilt in Harrow Road, but the licence was transferred to a new house when the arterial road was built. It has been renamed the *Brighton Run*.

109. The *Railway Tavern*, Pitsea, early this century. In 1856 the Railway Company stated that someone should build a small public house at Pitsea, as farmers and others complained of want of accommodation. (Information from letters relating to the building of Pitsea Station, lent to the author by Mr. E. Pettit in 1950.) The *Railway Tavern* which stood on land now covered by shops (on the north side of High Road, facing the market car park), was built in 1858-9 and was replaced by the present *Railway Hotel* between the two World Wars. The building then became two shops, one of which was the post office before its demolition. About 50 years ago the landlord of the *Railway Hotel* was Mr. Thorogood. He had a skittle alley at the back as well as an old-fashioned boiler in which he boiled hams.

110. The *Five Bells*, Vange in 1932, showing the old forge and cottages at the entrance to Bells Hill Road. The deeds go back to 1690, but the first mention of an inn known as the *Five Bells* occurs in the Alehouse Recognizance List in 1769, when William West was the landlord (E.R.O. Q/RLV 24/82). In 1791 William Aylett of Billericay, let the inn and the adjoining forge to Philip West at an annual rent of £14 8s. In the 17th century the building appears to have been a farm occupied by one Grace Samuel (E.R.O. D/Dch T 25).

111. The *Barge* Inn, Vange about 1906. Barge skippers from Vange Wharf were frequent customers here. Originall[y a] private house, the first inn here had the sign of the 'man with seven wives'. The innkeeper was called Wife and the si[gn] probably referred to the number of people in his family (Miller, *The Trade Signs of Essex*, 1887). On 2 September 1[xxx] an unknown man, described in Vange church register as a 'stranger', was found dead in an outhouse at the Seven Wiv[es] (E.R.O. D/P 298). The tarred timber outhouses and stables where the body was found stood on the west corner of [Bells] Hill Road. Inquests were sometimes held in the inn and the stables were used as a mortuary. There was also a pond nearby.

# XI Agriculture

Agriculture was practically the only occupation of the inhabitants of the Basildon area until the beginning of this century. In the 19th century Laindon Manor was described as being 'in fine corn country'. Many sheep were kept on the marshes for their wool and an extremely hard cheese was made from ewe's milk known as 'white meat'. It ceased to be made after the 18th century. Thomas Dowre of Pitsea in his will of 1556 left to his sister Paget 'one hard cheese' (E.R.O. D/ABW 12/75).

12. Harvesting on Hunts Farm, Basildon, 1958. The Doodes family seen in this picture, were the last to farm the land which is now covered by the No. 2 Industrial Site.

113. Ploughing in Cottage Field Goldings Farm about 1921. The ploughman was Jack Stiles who lived in one of the cottages to the east of the *Five Bells*. The round about now covers the site of the cottages (no. 110) and Ramsay Drive and Macdonald Drive now cover part of the field.

114. Feeding the chickens on Merricks Farm, Vange about 1913. In the picture are the two daughters of Mr. A. J. senior, Miss E. Moss and Mrs. E. Thompson and his granddaughter, Muriel Thompson, standing in the chaseway to the farmhouse. The house was on the right and the two willow trees on the left stood by a large horse pond. A coin of Emperor Gratian (375 - 378 A.D.) was found here when the pond was drained.

15.   Carting corn on Goldings Farm, Vange, 1921.  Haven Close and The Slades now cover this field.

116.   Sheep dipping at Goldings Farm, Vange about 1908.  Sheep have always been kept on the marshland farms.  A. J. Moss, senior, is standing with his grandchild watching his son and farmhand, Bill Brazier dip sheep in a tub in the farmyard.

117.   Threshing on Goldings Farm, Vange about 1921.  Mr. A. J. Moss, junior (on the right), is talking to Mr. Keeling who owned the threshing tackle and traction engine.  Threshing was quite an event on the farm, taking two or three days to complete.  Some of the threshing tackle workers would sleep in the big farm barn.

# XII Industry & Trade

Until the 19th century nearly all the inhabitants of the Basildon area had been engaged in agriculture, but in 1880 brick making became a thriving industry in Vange. Mr. Robert Leabon Curtis bought Vange Hall and approximately 350 acres of land north and south of the railway. He bought equipment from his brickfield at Plaistow and established a brickfield on the marsh south of the railway. Seven million bricks were manufactured here each year. The earth used was excavated from the marsh and also from the top of Sandhills Field, north of the High Road. The excellent quality earth was washed into slurry and pumped down by heavy three-throw pumps through four-inch cast-iron pipes into wash backs in the brickyard and was then mixed with chalk, sand and ashes and moulded into stock bricks. A fleet of six 90-ton barges brought cargoes of ashes, coal, chalk and sand to the works. Mr. Curtis built the Brickfield Wharf on Vange Creek where the bricks were loaded. In 1914 the works were taken over by the military and after the First World War they were dismantled (information from the late Mr. A. P. Curtis). There was also a smaller brickyard owned by Messrs. Clarke, Nickolls and Coombs Ltd. This was situated in a field to the west of Wharf or Merricks Lane (now completely built over) and was dismantled at the same time as the larger works.

Some of the oldest business premises in Basildon were the village smithies. The last surviving smithy was at Bowers Gifford, where Mr. A. H. Markham gave up the ancient forge and moved to new premises built on the site of a small wooden farmhouse known as Hiltons Farm.

118. Vange Brickfield workers in the early 1900s.

119. Vange Wharf and Merricks Farm in the 1920s, showing one of Goldsmiths' 'ironpots' at the wharf. Fishing was [an] industry here in medieval times and the Domesday Survey of 1086 records a fishery at Vange. Between 1565 and 157[?] 100 cod, 200 ling and 1,000 harberdyne (cured cod) were landed here. Barges have sailed regularly from Vange for se[veral] centuries. In the early 18th century James Emberson Benton who lived at Merricks owned barges here. The late Alfr[ed] John Moss (the last farmer to live in Merricks Farmhouse) had a fleet of barges sailing from Vange Wharf.

120. (*right*) In the early 1920s there was much talk about Vange Water and there were tales of miraculous cures. The well was near wood on Brickhouse Farm in Fobbing, but as the site was on Vange Hall Estate, the latter received the notoriety. It was discovered by Mr. King, a Vange farmer, and was publicised by the licensee of the *Angel*, Islington, Mr. E. Cash, who set up the Vange Water Company in 1919. In 1924 a large advertising board appeared on the north side of the London Road, just past the *Vange Bells*, which announced 'The Vale of Health'. Its fame was shortlived and a small Grecian temple is all that now remains.

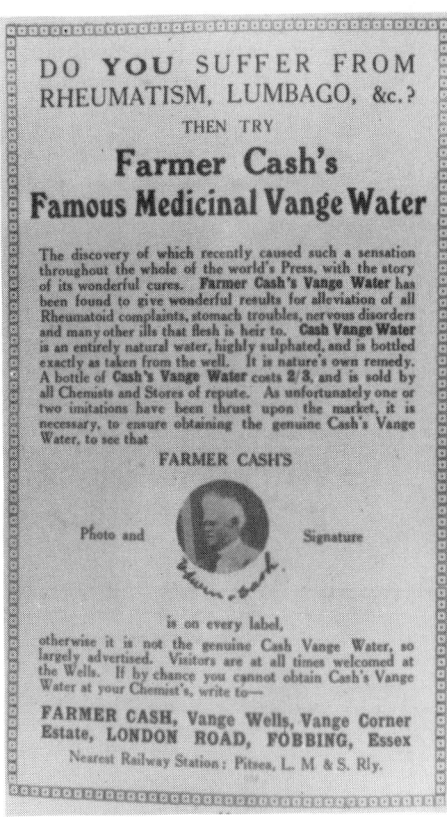

121. (*below*) The medicinal wells and pump room where Vange Water was obtained. It stood on the north side of the London Road. This photograph dates from 1924. Mr. E. Cash (in white coat) is standing on the extreme left. Note the motors.

122. The old forge, Bowers Gifford, early this century. stood on the north side of th London Road, to the east of the Rectory gate and was sa to date from 1600. Among many blacksmiths were Stephen Ransom in 1848 (White's *Gazetteer*) and George Thom Upson in 1890 (Kelly's *Dire tory*). The blacksmith in th picture is almost certainly M Ockendon. Note the lonely road leading to Thundersley

123. The Smithy, Dunton Road, Laindon, shortly after the First World War. It was said to be 200 years old and was still in use occasionally up to 1958. It had been in the same family for over 60 years. Thomas Newman came from Danbury to take over the forge which had belonged to the *Fortune of War*. There was mention of 'le Smithe' as early as 1444 (Guildhall MS. 10 312/127). In the photograph can be seen Gibbons' original coal lorry and on the right, Charles Buckenham of Sellars Farm mounting his horse.

The Five Bells, Vange.

124. The Blacksmith's the *Five Bells*, Vange ab 1907-8. One of the olde business premises in Var it is mentioned in a title deed of 1690 as 'a smith shop or fforge lately in tenure of Thomas Iore a now of the Churchward and Overseers of the par of Vange' (E.R.O. D/Dc T25). On the right is the open stable used by travellers stopping at the inn. The shop next doo was once a general store before becoming a butch shop. Note the pillar bo in the smithy wall.

# XIII Pitsea Windmill

A post mill stood above Howard Park until the end of the last century. There are various records of Pitsea millers. In 1586, John Hedgman was cautioned for grinding flour on Sunday. Despite pleading that it was necessary work he had to pay 12d. to the poor of Bowers Gifford as punishment (E.R.O. Archdeaconry transcripts). Another miller, John Wolmer left 16d. in his will of 1578 to buy Pitsea church a spade (E.R.O. 153 ER13). There are tombstones to various millers; James Stock, 1831; Robert Grout, 1869 and his son Robert Grout, 1878. Mrs. King, daughter of the last miller, John Willsmer, remembered her father using a long pole which he called a 'sacktackarigger' to swing the mill round to catch the wind. Willsmer leased the mill from H. G. P. Blencowe for £30 a year in 1881 and Blencowe had to spend £80 in repairs. Willsmer's account book was in use from 1879 to 1892. In 1881 he charged 16s. 6d. to grind a sack of barley. He let the mill house for £2 10s. a quarter. The mill was destroyed by fire at the end of the century. Sweeting, the village constable who lived at Sycamore Cottage (on the corner of Rectory Road) was on point duty when he saw flames coming from the mill. He ran all the way from Vange *Bells* to Pitsea to knock up the miller. (His daughter told the author that he had to lie flat on the floor to recover.) In any case there was little that could be done to save the mill as the nearest fire engine was at Billericay. Bricks from the burnt-out mill were used to build Pound Lane mission. The mill house survived for some years until it too was destroyed by fire. It had been in use as a children's holiday home: King Edward's Holiday Home. Children from London, whose parents were able to afford it, paid 5s. a week for their holiday. There is no known picture of the mill.

125. *(left)* Mill Lane, Pitsea, later known as The Ch
The lane which originally led to Pitsea Windmill ran
Rectory Road on the north side of Howard Crescen

126. *(below)* This picture is a copy of an old photo
on glass and shows the last Pitsea miller, John Willsn
his wife and some of their family outside their shop
White House, Pitsea, about 1890 (see nos. 40 & 41).
was also a baker and his bakery was at the back of th
shop. This also served as the only grocery store in th
village. One of his sons delivered bread over a wide a
in the district.

# XIV Water Supplies

There were no essential services in Basildon at the turn of the century. No gas, electricity, piped water supply or sanitation.

After the late R. L. Curtis established the Vange Brickworks, he built Vange Hall Cottages near the church in 1883. It is said that a local firm of haulage contractors used to fetch water in dry weather from Laindon Wash where a stream flowed across Wash Road and sell it to the inhabitants of these cottages.

Most Pitsea people washed in rain water collected from the roofs. Therefore the weekly wash presented a problem in dry weather. The tenants of four tiny cottages known as Bedlam Row in the High Road (near the entrance to Rectory Road) had to fetch water for washing day from the pond at the back of the village bakery, in dry weather. Drinking water was obtained from the pump on Gun Hill. The well at Pitsea Hall was destroyed by the railway. It was rediscovered by accident when someone nearly fell down it in the goods yard of Pitsea Station. Water for the station was brought from Low Street Station and to save walking to the pump it was sometimes stolen at night by nearby householders. In 1905 the first piped water supply was laid in the main road in Vange and Pitsea only. Most people had to fetch their water from standpipes in the road; only a few of the larger houses had the luxury of private supplies.

In January 1907, the first meeting of the Parochial Sanitary Committee of Vange, Pitsea and Bowers Gifford (an advisory committee to Billericay Rural District Council) was held and it was agreed to charge private meter holders 1s. 9d. per thousand gallons of water. In March 1908 control passed out of local hands when the Committee approved the decision of Billericay Council to hand over the supply to the Southend Waterworks Company and on 7 November 1907 it had been recommended that Pitsea pump be dismantled and the fittings sold (Minutes of the Pitsea, Vange and Bowers Gifford Sanitary Committee, in the author's possession).

In 1896 a company proposed to supply Laindon, Lee Chapel, Langdon Hills and Great and Little Burstead with gas and water. Within the next three years all they did was to supply some cottages at Little Burstead, sink a well and build the *Laindon* Hotel. However, the water supply was unsatisfactory and the medical officer of health said some substance had entered the tank and made the water unfit for drinking purposes. The pipes had not been laid properly and when the pump broke down there was no supply. A public enquiry was held at the *Laindon* Hotel by the Board of Trade in 1899. It was stated that in its first year not a penny had been subscribed; there had been no trading and no public issue of capital.

At this enquiry the Rector of Laindon and Basildon, the Rev. Carpenter said that some of his parishioners knew what it was to drink pond water. Asked where the cottages were that had only pond water he answered, 'all of them except those who come to my pump' (Southend Library, Reference Section, Petre

Newscuttings 1.029 3 ESS). The population of the village at this time was about five hundred.

In 1908 a Billericay postman, who walked 16 miles daily, retired. His round had included Basildon and he regularly pumped up the day's supply of water for the Rectory at Basildon before returning to Billericay.

127.   Water carrier on Church Hill, Langdon Hills.  This was the only supply for the village and the charge was ½d. a pail.  The water came from a well behind cottages in Dry Street.

128. Pitsea parish pump, last century. It stood on Gun Hill, at the entrance to Eversley Road and was the only water supply for miles around. It was in use until about 1905 when mains water was laid on, and standpipes were put in the roads near the houses. The building of Pitsea Factory on the marsh was said to have caused the well to fail. Water was then only available at certain times and the pump was kept locked. Sometimes the villagers had to rise in the early hours of the morning to obtain water and great hardship resulted. The baker, John Willsmer used the water from here for his breadmaking. A meeting of the Vange and Pitsea Sanitary Committee recommended on 7 November 1907 that the pump be dismantled and the fittings sold. (Information from the Minutes of the Pitsea, Vange and Bowers Gifford Sanitary Parochial Committee in the author's possession.)

129. The trunk of a sycamore tree had grown round this pump behind St. Gabriel's Church (photograph 1960) nearly covering it. The pump was a relic from the days when Shophouse Farm, or the Rectory as it was latterly known, had its own water supply. This was a luxury when nearly all Pitsea people had to fetch their water from the pump on Gun Hill. In 1907 the Rectory had a piped supply connected from the main at Hovefields Pumping Station and it was one of the first houses in Pitsea to have a private, piped water supply (Minutes of the Pitsea, Vange and Bowers Gifford Sanitary Parochial Committee).

130. Workers at Vange Waterworks. They seem more intent on having their photograph taken, than on work. There was a pumping station to the west of The Meads.

131. People came from a wide area to Merricks Farm (Riverside Farm) to buy water from the well. They paid 1d. a and carried the pails on yokes a quarter of a mile up Wharf Lane to the village. A late resident of Basildon remembere fetching water from this well and carrying it round to sell. When Pitsea Factory was built, about 1906, the well dried The pump can be seen on the extreme right of the photograph, not in its original position as it was no longer used. N the horseshoes on the tree, the earth closet and the henhouse in the background. The two grandchildren of the late A Moss, senior, are saying 'good night', the little girl is trying to kiss her reluctant cousin!

# XV Travel & Transport

Until the advent of the railway, the area of Basildon New Town was an isolated one. The nearest towns were Chelmsford and Romford. People travelled to town by carrier's cart. George Bettis, a Pitsea shopkeeper was also a carrier in 1855; his van travelled to Chelmsford every Friday (Kelly's *Directory*). In 1828 stage coaches were running through Vange and Pitsea.

The coming of the railway to Brentwood was such a novelty that one old farm labourer, Dick Wife, told the author's father that he walked from Vange to Brentwood just to see the trains. Dick died early this century.

Within two months of the passing of an act authorising the building of the London, Tilbury and Southend Railway in 1852 the landowners were instructed as to what land would be required by the Railway Company. John Oxley Parker of Woodham Mortimer Place conducted negotiations with the engineers and solicitors on behalf of Sir Charles Smith, Lord of the Manor of Vange, the Rev. George Heathcote, and the Hon. Payan Dawnay who held land at Pitsea. Originally the planned line was to run through Vange and Pitsea, near to the main road. A deviation from this in 1853 had to be approved by the justices. The changes in the route plan meant that Goldings and Riverside (Merricks) next to Vange Wharf just escaped destruction. At Pitsea Hall buildings had to be demolished and the line came almost to the windows of the house. In March 1854 it was agreed to pay £500 to Sir Charles Smith and £50 to the tenant at Vange. At Pitsea Hall £600 was paid for the land and £1,650 for the removal and rebuilding of the farm buildings (The Oxley Parker Papers, Lt. Col. J. Oxley Parker, D.L., M.A.).

In March 1855 a single line was in use and the line was doubled by the end of June. The author's grandfather, the late A. J. Moss, then aged about 12 years old, was surprised when his father (who farmed Barstable Hall) came to fetch him from Gravesend by train. When he had left home to go to school the line had only reached Stanford-le-Hope and now they could travel all the way to Pitsea by train. In 1888 the Upminster Line was completed to Pitsea and a new station was built there. Laindon station was built at the same time. In 1912 the old London, Tilbury and Southend Railway Company was absorbed by the Midland Railway which was then combined to form the London, Midland and Scottish Railway.

In 1900 the Campbell family had moved to Pitsea. They started a business with a horse-drawn cab, and then progressed to motors until they had a thriving coach hire business. This ceased about 1962.

The first regular bus service to Southend was run by the Westcliff Motor Services, Ltd., about 1920. The buses came to the *Barge* at Vange and the fare was 1s. 9d. return.

132.   Pitsea Station, early this century.  Roads were bad and motors scarce, so that for long and short journeys people travelled by train.  In the early years of this century there were about nineteen trains to London daily and the return fare was 3s. 6d.  A visit to Southend cost 10d. return and a season ticket to Southend cost £3 15s., quarterly.

133. (*above*) The staff at Pitsea Station in 1910. Notice the Nestle's chocolate machines against the wall in the background.

134. (*right*) A porter at Pitsea Station in 1910. Unfortunately his name is unknown.

135. The Railway Station at Pitsea and the Railway Cottages in the early 1900s. The Station-master's house is in the middle of the picture. Names of the railway staff who lived in the cottages, from left to right, are Spurgeon, Coulson, Boughtwood, Hughes, Chinnery, King, Wallace, Harrison and the Station-master, Mr. Puncher.

136. Pitsea Station, showing the Tilbury Line, built in the 1850s. Note the steam train, and Pitsea Hall on the left of the picture. The first station was to have been at Vange in the lane leading to the wharf, but the farmers did not favour this site. In 1854, at a meeting held at Pitsea a new site was chosen at Pitsea Hall. £150 was paid for half an acre of additional land and £50 for a fence along the road. The tenant had to move his corn from the barn, which was to be demolished and he received £20 in compensation. The first station was to be west of the present one, on the site of the goods yard seen in this picture (The Oxley Parker Papers).

137. An outing by horse-drawn brake, about 1910. Mr. J. W. Campbell is standing by the horses.

138. Pitsea Congregational Church outing in 1920. Note the 12 mile per hour speed restriction written on the vehicle's chassis. First left (seated), Mr. Plummer, second left (standing), J. W. Campbell, second from the left seated (in trilby hat), Mr. Upson, gentleman standing (white beard), Mr. Lewis, lady in black hat, second from the right is Mrs. Lewis, on Mr. Lewis' left, Mrs. Freeman, lady in glasses on right of lady in white hat is Mrs. Lamb.

139. Saunders' bakery cart and pony, taken about 1919. The bakery stood not many yards to the east of the *Barge* inn, and on the same side of the road.

140. Saunders' bakery delivery van in the 1920s at Pitsea. Standing by the van are Norman Grimwade and A. Waylett, with Mr. Upson in the background.

# XVI When Land Was Cheap

The agricultural depression of the late 19th century led to many farms in the Basildon area being sold for building. The farms were bought by speculators who divided the land into plots and then resold to make a quick profit. The company selling land at Vange and Pitsea gave free lunches at the sales, which were held frequently from 1901 to 1906, and were very popular, probably on account of the free liquor.

Some sales were difficult to complete because the purchasers became drunk at the marquees put up for the sales, tore up their contracts and threw the pieces out of the trains on their way home, for they had paid only a small deposit. Others bought cheap plots and forgot about them.

Plots on the Alexander Park Estate (Northlands Farm), 20 ft. by 250 ft., cost £8. A half acre was £30 and an acre sold for £50. Plots on the Brightside Estate, Pitsea, with frontage to the High Road from Howard Park to the *Bull* Inn cost £35. On Highlands Estate, Vange (stated to be 150 ft. above sea level), plots 20 ft. by 100 ft. sold for as little as £5. A sale of plots on River View Estate, south of High Road from the *Barge* to the Working Men's Club, was held on 9 October 1907 in a marquee near the *Barge* Inn at 2 p.m. Prices were from £8 for a 20 ft. by 120 ft. plot. A 10% deposit was required when signing the contract and immediate possession was given. The balance was payable by 16 quarterly payments if desired. Although the catalogues stated that the roads were 'capital' most plots were some distance from them. They were 'formed free' but were in fact entirely unmade up and became quagmires in winter.

A few false sewer inspection chambers were put in some roads—but there was no hope of sanitation. The area was said to be one of the healthiest localities in England. There was no doctor at Pitsea (evidence of the healthiness of the area?!); the nearest doctors were at Wickford and Stanford-le-Hope.

As regards employment the sale particulars stated that the nearby 'important and extensive works of Kynocks for the manufacture of cordite, gun cotton, etc.,' employed about 700 people. There was also the British Explosives Company's factory on Pitsea Marshes, within 'an easy walk'. Nationalisation was also predicted. Land was cheap and workers would be able to have large gardens of their own and 'to a certain extent the wishes of many philanthropists will be fulfilled. Nationalisation in this part of the country will then become an established fact.'

In 1892 three land sales were held on 12 May, 8 June and 21 June at 2 p.m. each day for Langdon Hills and the Laindon Station Estate. The auctioneers issued London buyers with tickets at 2s. each including a luncheon on the estate.

Many of the plots remained derelict until the time the Basildon Development Corporation took over in 1949 (Refs. E.R.O. A 143; A 151).

141.   This is Mr. Foulgar, the Estate Agent (complete with top hat), who met prospective buyers at Laindon Station and took them on a tour of the area.

142.   A page from a sale catalogue of the Land Company of Cheapside, London, about 1906.  The caption reads 'popular, prosperous, picturesque, but no mention is made of the unmetalled roads shown in the illustrations. The picture, top left, shows the *Railway Tavern*, Pitsea. Top right is Thames Drive, Vange, which was on the south of the High Road. The picture, bottom right, taken from the railway, near the bridge crossing the High Road and looking north east shows Brickhouse Farm on the left and houses on the High Road (E.R.O. A 151).

**London, Tilbury, and Southend**
**RAILWAY TICKET.**

**LAINDON HILLS.**
**SPECIAL AUCTION LAND SALE,**
**Monday, October 18th, 1897.**
**FENCHURCH STREET to LAINDON.**
3 Class.    11 a.m. or 12.15 p.m. Train.

**London, Tilbury, and Southend**
**RAILWAY TICKET.**

**LAINDON HILLS.**
**SPECIAL AUCTION LAND SALE,**
**Monday, October 18th, 1897.**
**LAINDON to FENCHURCH STREET.**
2 Class.    5.41 p.m. or 7.45 p.m. Train.

143. London, Tilbury and Southend Railway ticket for the journey to the special land sales at Laindon and Pitsea, 18 October 1897. That year about one hundred and fifty plots of freehold land were offered for sale. A large company arrived by train and sat down to a 'capital lunch' and refreshments were handed round afterwards. About one hundred plots were sold and prices ranged from £70 10s. down to £11 10s. About 1906 the sale particulars stated that free tickets for Pitsea were issued any day (E.R.O. A 151).

# XVII Old Basildon People, Places & Miscellaneous Events

This section is limited by the number of photographs in the author's collection and those she could obtain from the kind people who helped in some way with the compilation of this book. It is hoped, however, that the pictures may give some impression of the country folk and the lives they led in the then quiet villages of Basildon in the late 19th and early years of this century.

144. Mrs. Tinworth of Rose Cottage, Dry Street, Langdon Hills, taken in about 1912 when she was 100 years old. She lived to be 102 years old. Her husband was a shoemaker and she was a dressmaker. She possessed the only clock in the district.

145. The Sach family outside their farm cottage off One Tree Hill, Langdon Hills, about 1900.

146. (*left*) The opening cere[...] at Pitsea Congregational Chur[...] Fete, about 1912. The little g[...] who is about to present the bouquet to the lady opening [...] fete is Miss W. P. Cook.

147. (*below*) The maypole dance at Pitsea Congregational Church Fete, about 1912.

148. (*left*) Pitsea Congregatio[...] Church, Gun Hill, now the Eli[...] Church. This replaced a tiny cottage (still inhabited) where [...] first Congregationalists met. U[...] last century it appears that ne[...] all the people in the Basildon a[...] belonged to the established Ch[...] One of the first nonconformis[...] churches began in a chapel tha[...] is now a small, one-storey tim[...] cottage on the south side of G[...] Hill opposite Eversley Road. [...] Pitsea miller, John Willsmer an[...] Mrs. Upson were responsible f[...] building and opening this tiny [...] place of worship for the Congr[...] gationalists about 1880. It wa[...] the only Congregational Churc[...] for miles and North Benfleet p[...] (owing to the distance from th[...] homes) used to stay at the cha[...] for the day, so they could atte[...] all the services. They brought [...] and tea was made for them on [...] tiny fireplace in the chapel. (Information from the late Mrs [...] King of Pitsea.)

149. Mrs. Willsmer, the wife of the Pitsea miller and [ba]ker, with two of her large family. She had about four[te]en children. The picture was taken about 1890. An [ol]d resident of Pitsea can remember her serving in the little [gr]ocery shop in the White House (see nos. 40 & 41) and [u]sing a beautiful shell to scoop up sugar.

150. Mrs. Howard, an old inhabitant of Vange in 1939. She lived in Woodbine Cottages, in the cottage on the right (see below). Note her sun bonnet.

[1]51. Woodbine Cottages, High Road, [V]ange. They stood on the north side [o]f the road to the west of the Working [M]en's Club. An old inhabitant in the [1]930s could remember when they were [q]uite new. They had been built about [1]838 and were demolished in 1958.

152. (*above*) The Rev. St. John F. C. Methuen, M.A., Rector of Vange from 1897 to 1931. He was very interested in rose growing at Vange Rectory. The site is now that of Vange Zoo.

153. (*below*) Mr. and Mrs. Samuel Wiseman, two old inhabitants of Vange, in 1922. Their combined ages were 175 years. This photograph appeared in the *Southend Standard* for 8 June, 1922. The little two roomed cottage which was their home stood at the top of the old Paynters Hill.

154. (*above*) Major Thomas Jenner Spitty of 'Hurlocks', Billericay, wearing his court dress as Deputy Lieutenant of Essex in 1881. He was the chief landowner in Bowers Gifford and built Shell Cottages next to Blue House Farm as a shooting box. Bowers Hall, built by an ancestor of his in 1828, displays the family coat of arms. Blue House Farm, Pitsea was largely rebuilt by another Thomas Spitty in 1806. The Spittys were originally cattle drovers from Y Spitty Yotwith in Cardiganshire (H. Richman, *Billericay and its High Street*) and became large landowners. They were connected with the Basildon district for 300 years. Major Spitty who was the last member of the family to be connected with Bowers, was born in 1812 and died in 1898. Many of the old Bowers and Pitsea people remembered him well. The estates were sold in 1917. His coach, dating from 1820, is preserved in Colchester Museum.

155. Alfred John Moss, the author's father, at the turn of the century. He is wearing the uniform of the Essex Yeomanry, to which he belonged. The photograph was taken on Merricks Farm, Vange. The Moss family farmed Luncies Farm, Hill Farm, Merricks Farm and Goldings Farm in Vange and Barstable Hall and Fairhouse Farm in Basildon. Moss Drive and Moss Close are named after the family.

156. An informal picture of the Moss family at Merricks Farm, Vange, about 1901. It was taken by the author's uncle who was a keen photographer. It shows two of the sons and two daughters of the late A. J. Moss, senior. Standing by the door is Mr. Leonard Moss, and in the centre of the picture are Miss Ethel Moss, Miss Ellen Moss and Mr. Benjamin Moss.

157. Workers on the way to Kynocks Explosives Factory, on the Thameshaven Marshes during the First World War.

158. Vange National Walking Race winners, of unknown date. The race was from Vange to Wickford and back, a distance of ten miles. The picture was taken outside Joe Collet's barber's shop, which was on the north side of High Road, Vange, near Kent View Road. From left to right are Joe Collet, Bill Blake, Fred Painter, two unidentified men, Ernie Campbell, unidentified man, Stan Cranfield, Jack Germany, unidentified man, and Kate Fuller (Mrs. Collet).

159.  A fancy dress dance at Pitsea School, 15 February 1923.  Note the oil lamps.

160.  J. W. Campbell's decorated cart in the Pitsea/Vange carnival, sometime in the 1930s.

161. Langdon Hills, 1830. The most picturesque spot in Basildon and long a favourite place for picnics. An 1820 ne
cutting (E.R.O. T/P 110/35) records a 'Fete Champetre' when 'a large and elegant party assembled on Langdon Hills f
the purpose of viewing from thence one of the most extensive prospects which this country affords'. After admiring t
view 'the company were summoned by the sound of a cheerful bugle admirably played by one of the gentlemen and s
down under a friendly oak to a cold collation'. After the meal the ladies 'dispersed in straggling parties over the hill, t
fair forms contrasting with the wild and sylvan scenery contributing not a little to its beauty'. The gentlemen who we
less energetic enjoyed various sorts of 'excellent wine'. 'But now Phoebus gently withdrew his effulgent rays and by h
decline warned the party to separate. They still lingered, however, till the shadows of evening closed the charming sc

162. Many Londoners owned weekend bungalo
in Laindon, Pitsea, Vange and Basildon. They we
in general rather primitive dwellings, with few, if
any, modern conveniences and were situated on
unmetalled roads. This photograph shows a typic
scene at Laindon Station during the 1920s or '30s
Weekenders are waiting for what was called the
'Sunday Night Special' to London.

THE BUNGALOW OF MR & MRS WATSON, HONEY POT LANE, BASILDON. 831.

163 & 164. In 1906 the middle-aged couple who lived here, Mr. and Mrs. Watson, were murdered. Their only water supply was from a pond, but dry weather forced them to collect water from another pond on Sawyers Farm. They were shot on the banks of the pond (164). Two brothers were accused of the murder and one confessed. Angry at someone else taking water from his pond, he shot the couple six times in a blind rage. He was found guilty, but his brother was acquitted. The murder spot was particularly isolated; it is now near the town centre (E.R.O. T/P 181/2/175). A news report added that if the police possessed a motor car the prisoners would have been held the same day, instead of waiting until the next morning before they were certain enough to make arrests. The report read the district is such a remote one that a motor car was really necessary and the tragedy suggested the desirability of the chief constable being supplied with such means of progression, ready for any emergency' (Petre Newscuttings, Southend Library 1.029.3 Ess).

165. The view from Pitsea Church Hill in the 1920s. The old *Railway Tavern* can be seen to the left of a tall tree on right of the photograph. On the extreme left is a field, now the site of the *Railway Hotel,* which replaced the *Railway Tavern*; the end of Station Lane and an avenue of trees, Northlands Drive. The open space between this and the *Railway Tavern* is now the shopping and market area and car park. In the foreground is Church Hill Path.

166. One of the many unmetalled roads with small timber-framed bungalows that were typical of the district before the coming of the Ne[w] Town.